DESPERATELY SEEKING B**KSY

XAVIER TAPIES

GINGKO PRESS

THE EARLY YEARS

We know that Banksy got going with the graffiti gang in the Barton Hill area of Bristol, but he was never really a graffiti artist. From the get-go he was someone who had stumbled and developed a bigger vision of how the street could be commandeered to amazing effect. These early works – from 2002 – laid down themes that would live through his work to the present day. From the punning language, to the sending-up of authority figures and, most significantly, some highly politicised anti-war messages, Banksy was launched on several fronts very early on.

THE MILD MILD WEST

GORILLA IN A PINK MASK

THERE IS ALWAYS HOPE

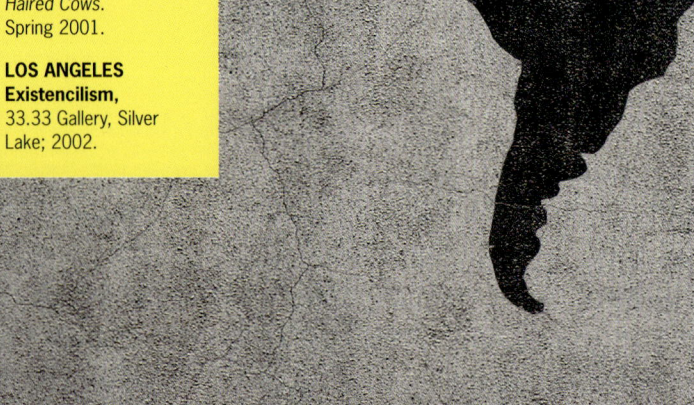

BANKSY EARLY YEARS

We know very little about the early years. Banksy is mixing it with various graffiti artists in Bristol, Inkie and Robert Del Naja included. At first only the signature is stencilled. Then we have the switch to using the stencil for the main image and the use of satire and humour emerges and Bristol begins to love *The Mild, Mild West*. And then Banksy moves to London and things begin to snowball. It is in London that we first see Banksy using street art to convey his political messages.

EXHIBITIONS AND INTERVENTIONS

BRISTOL
Severnshed, Bristol, *Flower Thrower* (in a Crowd), *Monkey Riding Bomb;* March 2000.

LONDON
Open Air, Cargo, Rivington Street, Shoreditch, *Speak Softly But Carry a Big Can of Paint, Billboard Monkeys, Spiky Haired Cows.* Spring 2001.

LOS ANGELES
Existencilism, 33.33 Gallery, Silver Lake; 2002.

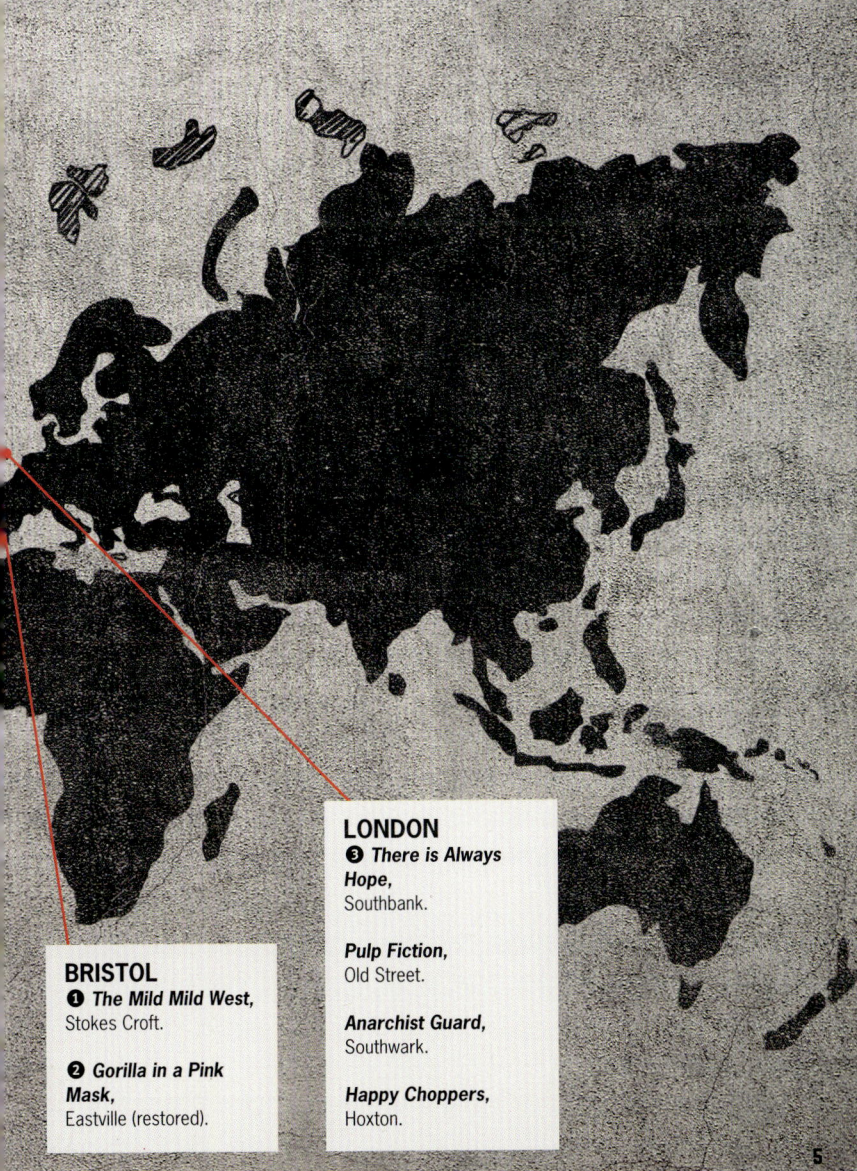

BRISTOL
❶ *The Mild Mild West,*
Stokes Croft.

❷ *Gorilla in a Pink Mask,*
Eastville (restored).

LONDON
❸ *There is Always Hope,*
Southbank.

Pulp Fiction,
Old Street.

Anarchist Guard,
Southwark.

Happy Choppers,
Hoxton.

1

THE MILD MILD WEST

"I didn't become a graffiti artist so I could have someone else tell me what to do."
Banksy, quoted in *Time Out*.

One of the earliest works by Banksy which still survives. It was painted shortly before Banksy left Bristol for London. It might look a bit like a stencil, but this is in fact one of Banksy's last freehand works. It does show, however, that at the core of every Banksy is a brilliantly witty, visual idea which can operate on many levels.

WHERE IS IT ?
STOKES CROFT,
BRISTOL,
UK.
STILL THERE!

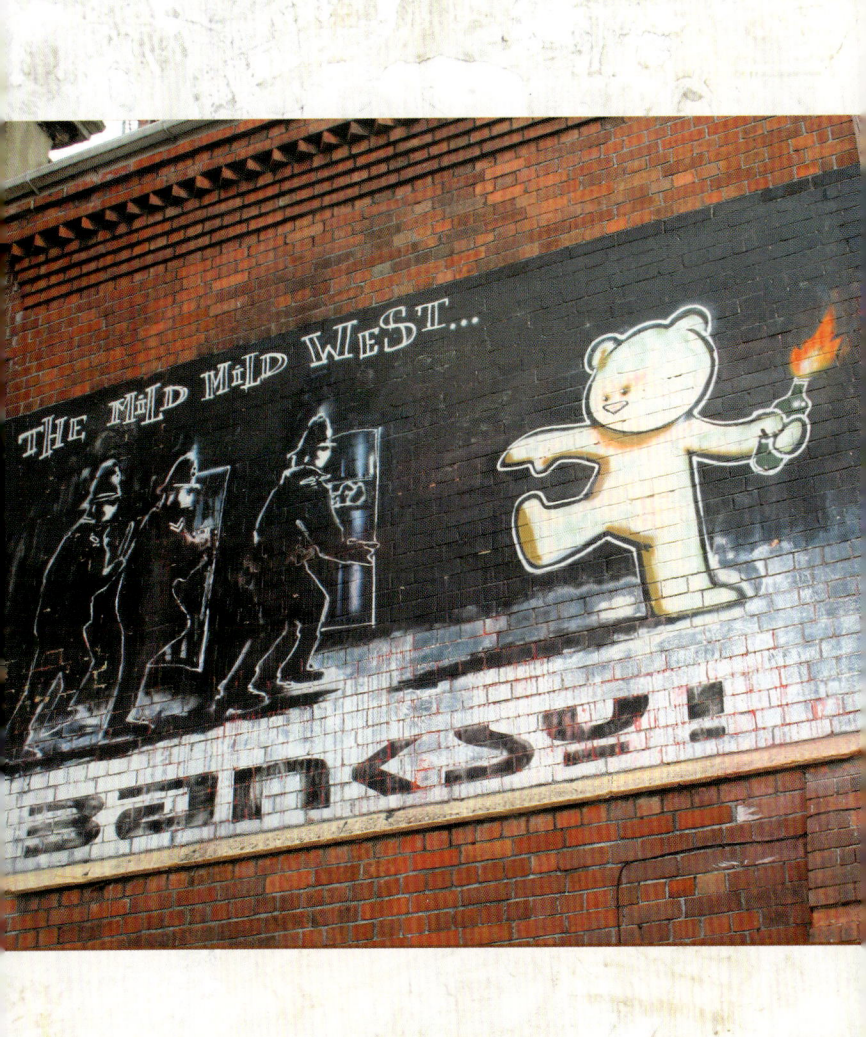

2

GORILLA IN PINK MASK

"I thought it was worthless.
I didn't know it was valuable.
That's why I painted over it."
Representative from the
Muslim Cultural Centre, Bristol.

At the time that it was painted, this was just a bit of fun by Banksy. This time he is sending up the idea of masculinity: our mega-strong, brutal gorilla is really a big softy, and rather shy, hiding behind a very feminine electric pink mask. Banksy was to repeat this idea of juxtaposing pink against a monochromatic stencil many times.

WHERE IS IT ?
EASTVILLE,
BRISTOL,
UK.
WAS PAINTED OVER IN 2011 AND
HAD TO BE RESTORED. NOW A
SHADOW OF ITS FORMER SELF.

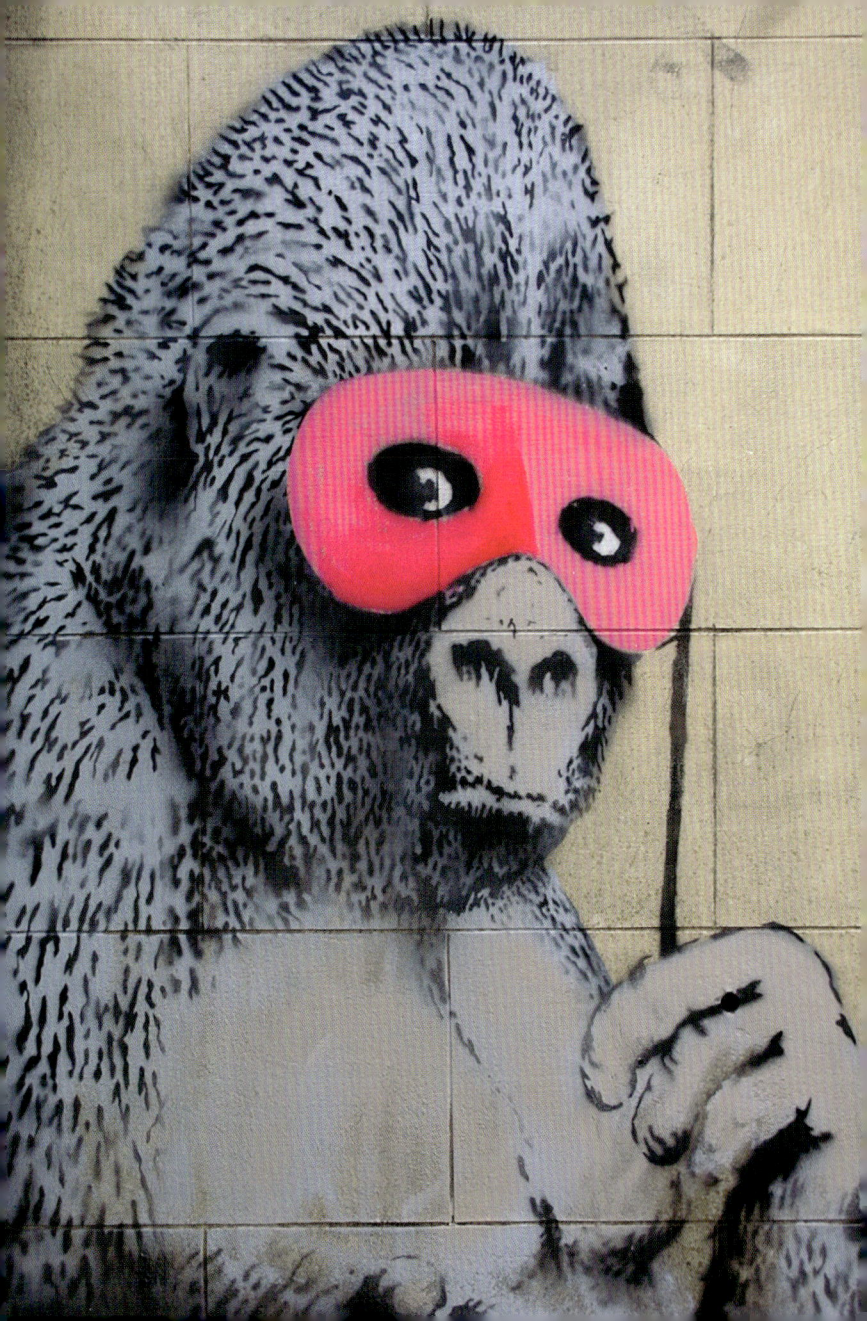

❸

THERE IS ALWAYS HOPE

"Banksy paints over the line between aesthetics and language."
Shepard Fairey

This piece, still one of Banksy's most popular images (if sales of canvases and t-shirts are a measure) reveals a hugely sensitive side to Banksy and also sees him using the image of a child to devastating effect. Images of children were to prove a rich vein for him, carrying with them, as they do, big emotional punch.

WHERE IS IT ?
SOUTHBANK,
LONDON,
UK.
EAST STAIRCASE LEADING UP
TO WATERLOO BRIDGE.

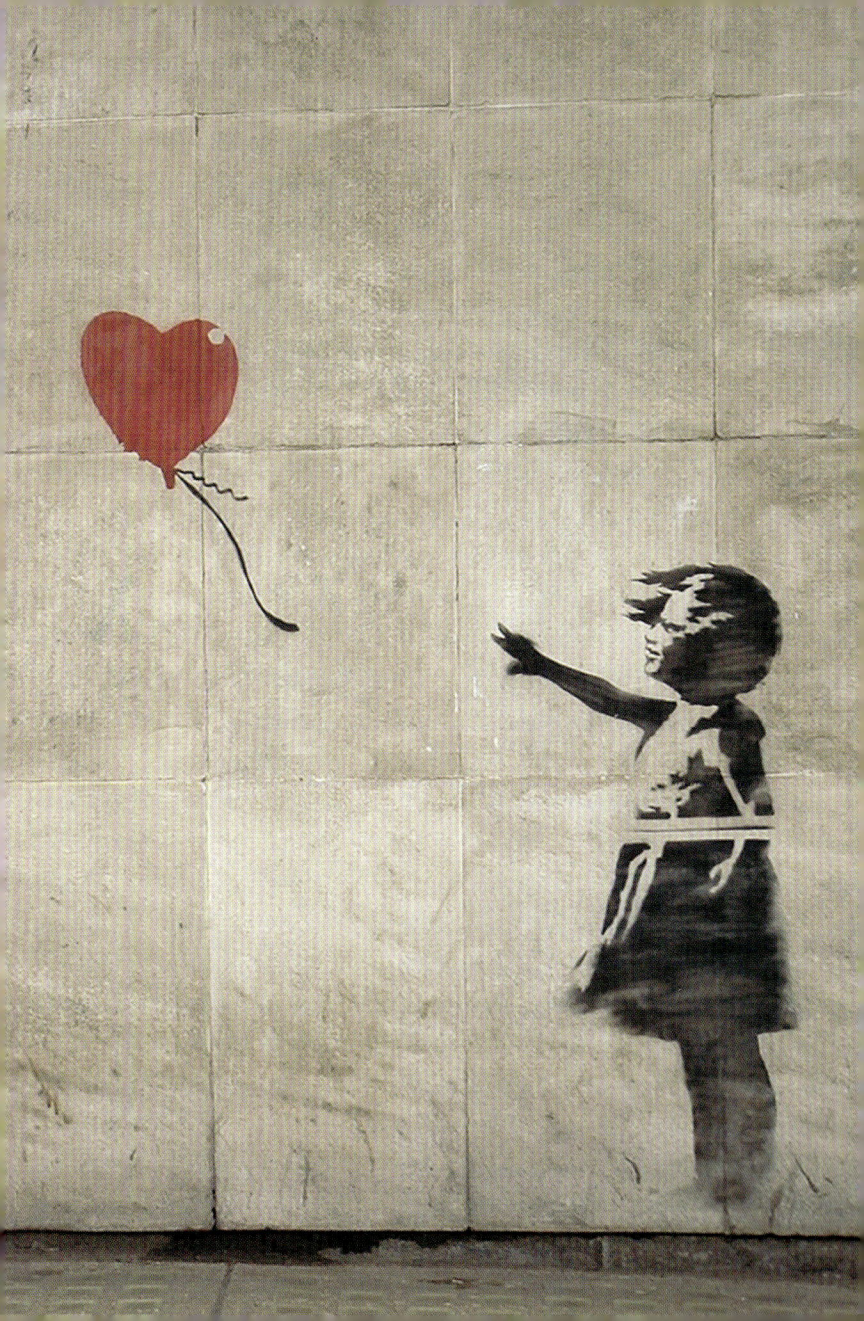

2003-2004

One of Banksy's most powerful works – *Flower Thrower* – emerged in 2003, and highlighted his preoccupation with the plight of the Palestinians on the West Bank and Gaza Strip. At this point Banksy was still creating in Bristol, the west country and London, in addition to the Middle East. During this period we see the first eloquent use of the rat, a nod to French street art maestro Blek. We also see the emergence of a second major political strand to his work: surveillance and the overweening power of the state over the individual.

THE GRIM REAPER
RAGE: THE FLOWER THROWER
BECAUSE I'M WORTHLESS
KISSING COPPERS
WHAT ARE YOU LOOKING AT?

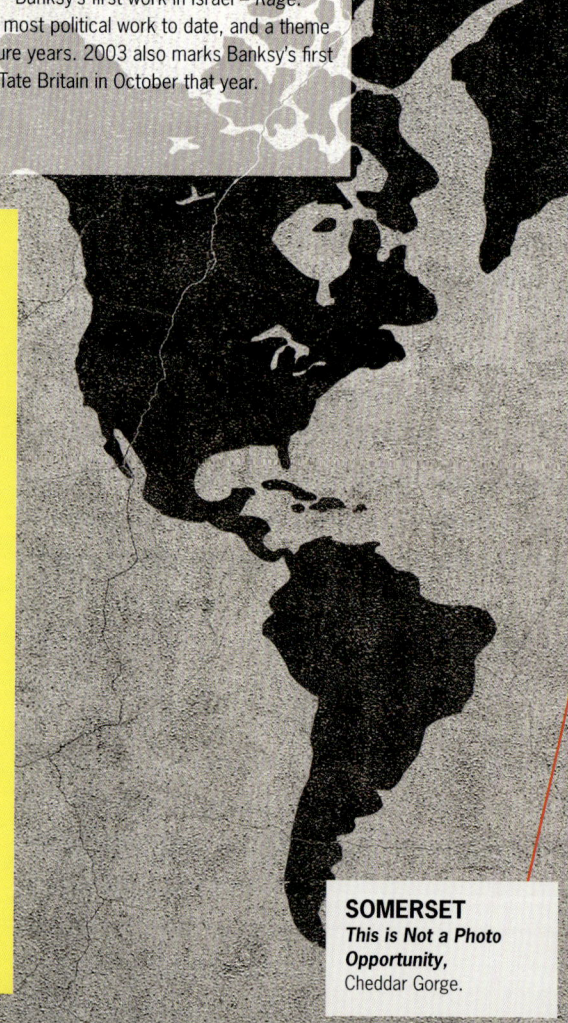

2003-2004

Banksy is still mostly working in the UK, with works appearing in his home town of Bristol, in London and a couple of works in Brighton, on the English south coast. 2003 however marks a significant development – Banksy's first work in Israel – *Rage: The Flower Thrower*, his most political work to date, and a theme he would return to in future years. 2003 also marks Banksy's first gallery intervention – at Tate Britain in October that year.

EXHIBITIONS AND INTERVENTIONS

LONDON
Turf War,
Dalston;
21st –23rd July 2003.

Tate Britain,
Millbank, London.
Painting with police tape stuck to it, hung by Banksy in the gallery;
October 2003.

Diana £10 notes,
scattered at the Notting Hill Carnival; last weekend in August, 2004.

PARIS
Mona Lisa Smiley Face,
Louvre, Paris;
2004.

SYDNEY
Semi-Permanent,
Alexandria, Sydney (part of a larger exhibition, including Shepard Fairey);
May 2003.

SOMERSET
This is Not a Photo Opportunity,
Cheddar Gorge.

LONDON
❸ *Because I'm Worthless,* Clerkenwell.

Drunken Angel, London Bridge.

Thug for Life Bunny, Shoreditch.

Tourist Information, Bethnal Green.

❺ *What Are You Looking At?,* Marble Arch Station.

OTHER LOCATIONS VISITED BY BANKSY

MELBOURNE
April, 2003

CHICAGO
May, 2004

BERLIN
July, 2004

BETHLEHEM
❷ *Rage: The Flower Thrower,* garage forecourt.

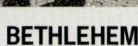

BRIGHTON
Dynamite Ice Cream, Brighton Beach.

❹ *Kissing Coppers,* Trafalgar Street. Original sold and replaced by a copy.

BRISTOL
❶ *The Grim Reaper,* *Thekla* hull, (now in M-Shed), Bristol Docks.

15

1

THE GRIM REAPER

"We have no intention of selling the Banksy."
Owners of the *Thekla*, Bristol.

Painted directly onto the hull of *Thekla*, a party boat anchored in Bristol harbour, this haunting image is at first hard to decipher. Given its context, and what wc know of Banksy's sardonic sense of humour, it's quite funny to show the reaper in a location where everyone is getting loved-up, dancing, thinking they will live forever.

WHERE IS IT ?
ORIGINALLY ON THE HULL OF THE
THEKLA, BRISTOL HARBOUR.
NOW PRESERVED IN THE M SHED.
BRISTOL,
UK.

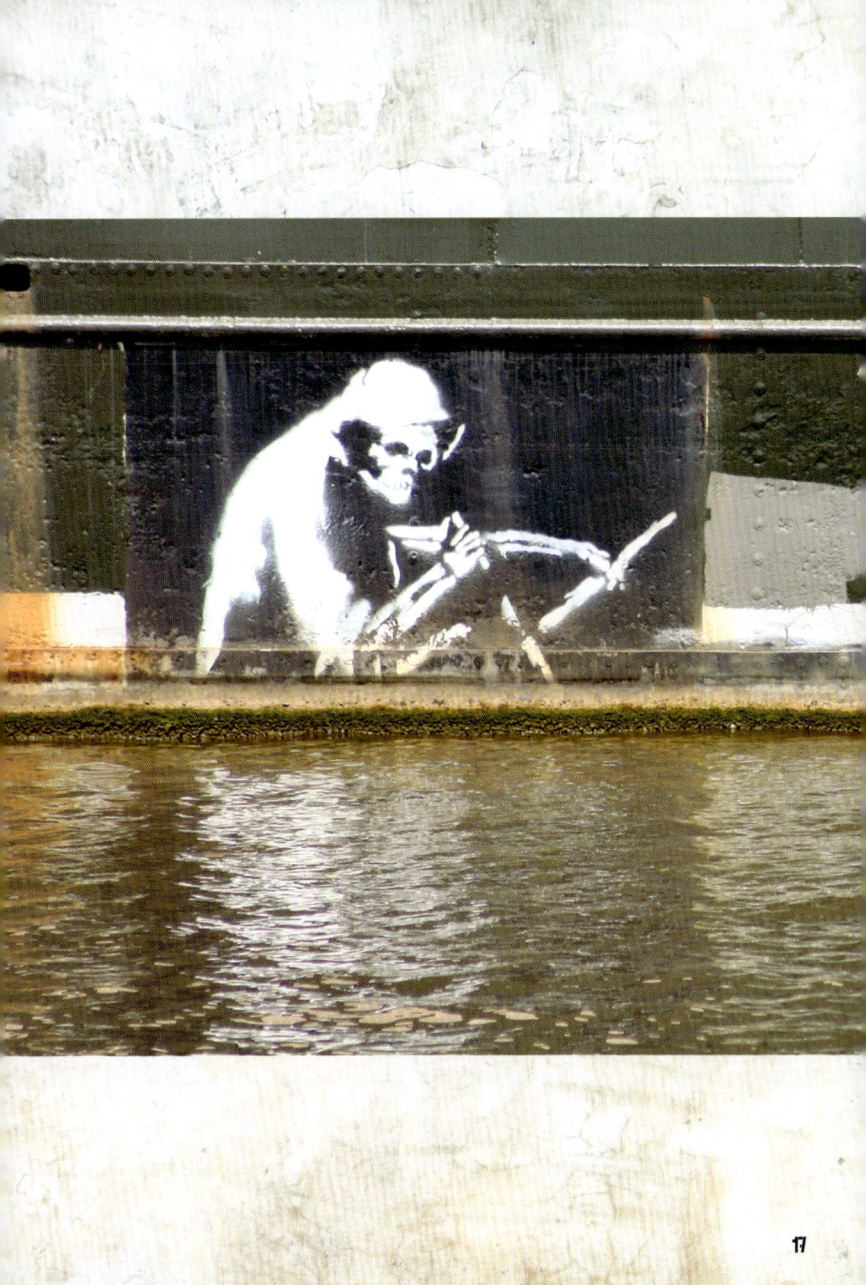

❷

RAGE:
THE FLOWER THROWER

"The innocent imprisoned. Movement restricted. Trade suffocated. Homes demolished. Human rights abuses are rife in Israel and the Occupied Palestinian Territories."
Amnesty International, 2016.

The Israeli-Palestinian conflict is one which has pre-occupied Banksy, and where he has taken considerable risks, to both highlight it to the wider world and to use his artistic powers to try and express a way of ending the deadlock. *Flower Thrower* might well be his best-known and evocative single work, not least because it formed the cover of Banksy's seminal *Banksy Wall and Piece* book.

WHERE IS IT ?
BIET SAHOUR,
BETHLEHEM,
PRESERVED
UNDER PERSPEX.

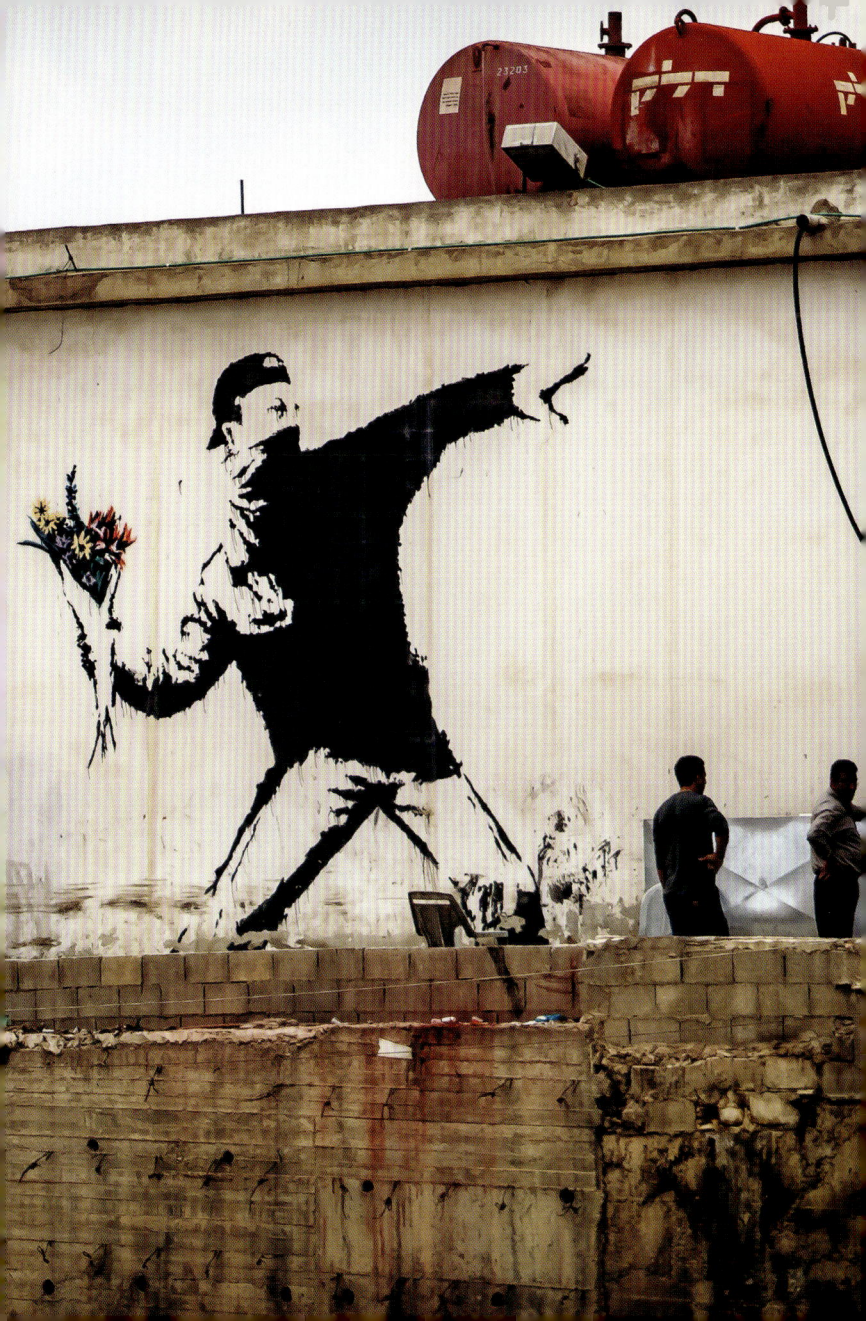

3

BECAUSE I'M WORTHLESS

"There's no way round it – commercial success is a mark of failure for a graffiti artist."
Banksy, interviewed in *Village Voice*.

A delicious send-up of the nauseating, ubiquitous, vapid L'Oreal campaign strap-line. That stream of tedium which saw various models repeat the moronic line "Because I'm worth it" over and over and over again, is here transformed into a brilliant piece of wit.

WHERE IS IT ?
CLERKENWELL,
LONDON,
UK

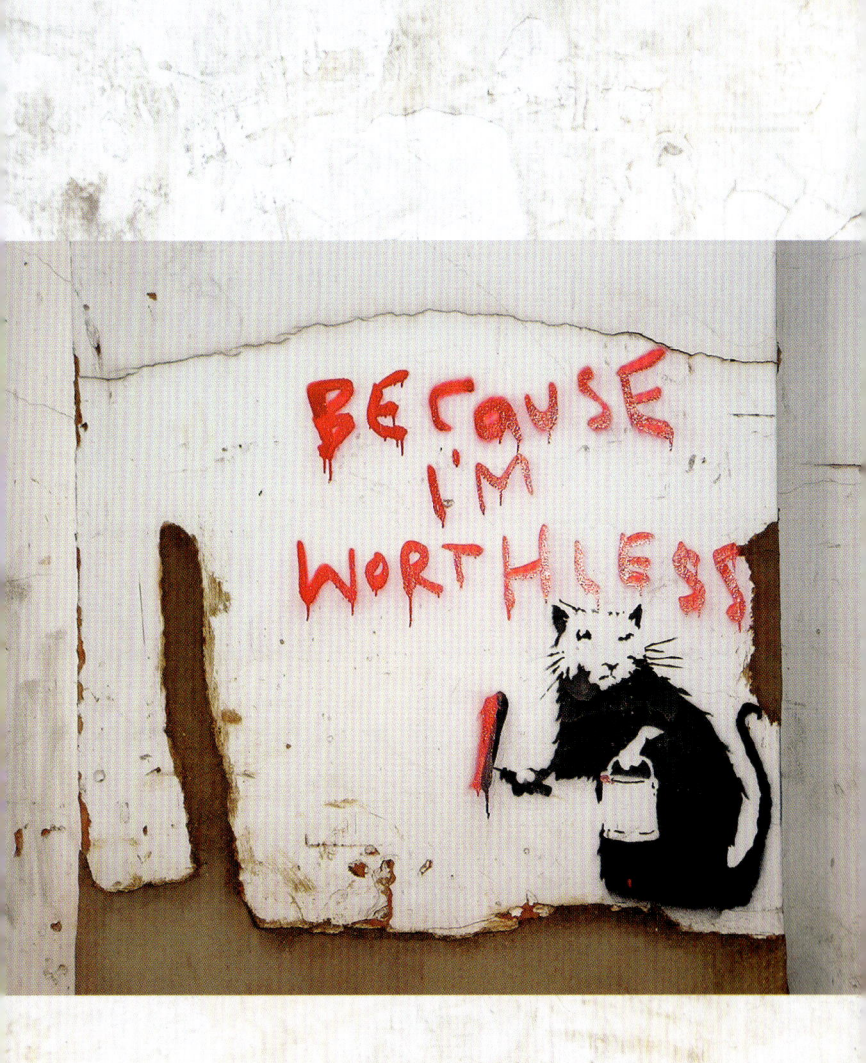

4

KISSING COPPERS

"When he put it on the pub it belonged to the pub and, if it is sold, all the money will go back to the pub."
Chris Seward, owner of the Prince Albert.

Banksy has form in cocking a snook at establishment figures and the police are in good company with the Queen and Royal Guards, to name a few. This piece is perfect as a celebration of tolerance in a city noted for its gay-friendly vibe since the 1960s.

WHERE IS IT ?
ORIGINALLY TRAFALGAR STREET,
BRIGHTON,
UK.
REMOVED FROM PUB WALL AND SOLD TO
PRIVATE BUYER AT AUCTION IN MIAMI IN 2014.
A REPLICA HAS NOW REPLACED THE ORIGINAL.

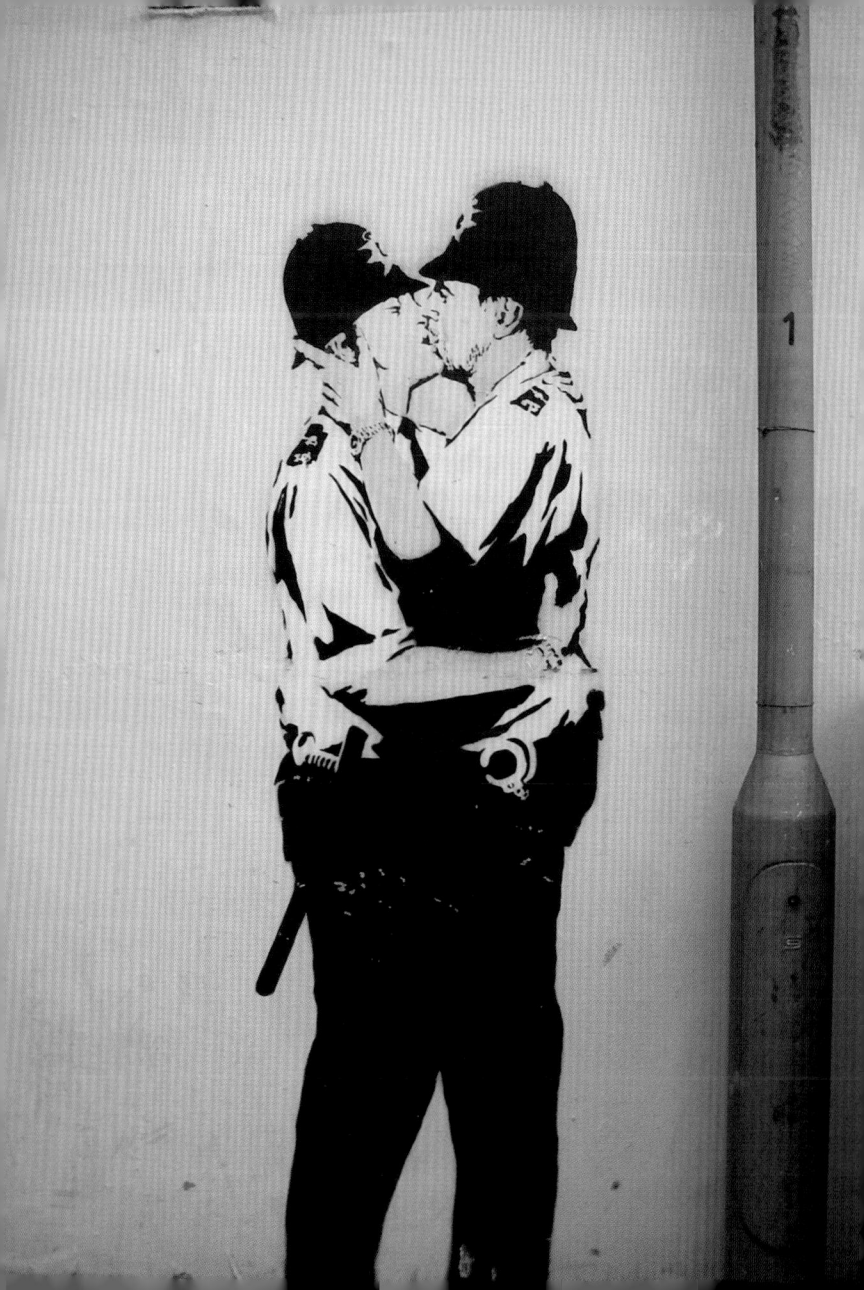

❺

WHAT ARE YOU LOOKING AT?

"My anxiety is that we don't sleepwalk into a surveillance society."
Richard Thomas, UK information Commissioner, interview in *The Times*.

Banksy has always had a good nose for authoritarian power-grabs. The oppressive nature of constant surveillance which crept up on the British people by stealth was always going to be a ripe subject for him. The tedious authorities of course painted this piece over, despite its wit and elegance. They also quietly removed the very stupidly placed camera. Game, set and match: Banksy.

WHERE IS IT ?
MARBLE ARCH STATION,
LONDON,
UK.
HAS BEEN PAINTED OVER AND THE SECURITY
CAMERA HAS ALSO BEEN REMOVED.

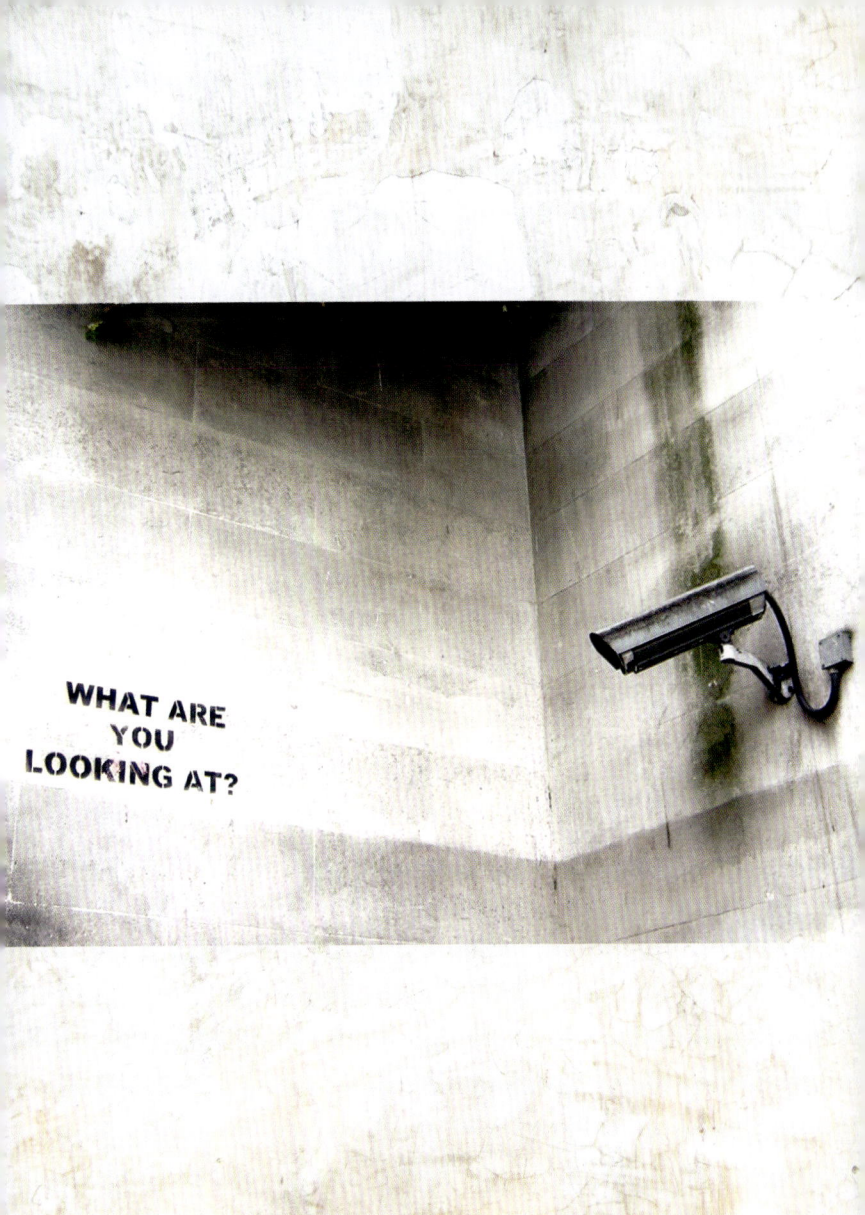

2005-2006

Banksy is starting to become a significant figure in the UK. *The Guardian* in particular latched onto him. His works are sought out by London hipsters. The themes of surveillance and druggy cops are continued in his work. The biggest shift in 2005 is his Guantanamo stint at Disneyland in California, which hugely raises his profile in the US. Now Hollywood A-listers start collecting him. Back in London he creates the image (based on Sweeping It Under the Carpet) that was later to achieve his all-time highest sale price, *Keeping it Spotless*, with Damien Hirst.

GUANTANAMO
SNORTING COPPER
BOY AT THE BEACH
WELL HUNG LOVER
SWEEPING IT UNDER THE CARPET

2005-2006

This is the period when Banksy's work steps up several gears and becomes truly international. Banksy creates significant works in London, his very influential series along the West Bank Wall and in Los Angeles.

More museum interventions take place in 2005 – at the Louvre in Paris and at the Metropolitan, Brooklyn, MOMA and Natural History museums in New York.

EXHIBITIONS AND INTERVENTIONS

LOS ANGELES
Barely Legal,
Los Angeles. Includes
Elephant in the Room and
Queen Victoria as Lesbian;
16th Sept 2006.

**Guantanamo Bay
Detainee,**
Disneyland, Anaheim;
Sept 2006.

NEW YORK
Banksy interventions at
various museums, including
a Warhol-style Tesco 'value'
soup can, which hung
in MOMA for three days
before being detected;
2005.

PARIS
Banksy plants his version
of the Mona Lisa, featuring
an 'acid' face, in the Italian
Grand Masters room in the
Louvre; 2005.

LOS ANGELES
No More Heroes,
Melrose Avenue.

*I'm Out of Bed and
Dressed,*
Melrose Avenue.

LONDON
Up Periscope,
Bethnal Green.

❶ **Guantanamo,**
Islington.

Photographer Rat,
Islington.

Thug for Life,
Clerkenwell.

❷ **Snorting Copper,**
Waterloo.

❺ **Sweeping it Under the Carpet,**
Hoxton.

Graffiti Removal Hotline,
Islington.

LONDON
Crude Oils,
Westbourne Grove.
Banksy-subverted *Monet Water Lillies* and *Hopper's Nighthawks*;
October 2005.

Sotheby's, London. Kate Moss silkscreen prints achieve £50,400;
19th Oct 2006.

UK
Banksy replaces some 500 Paris Hilton CDs in record shops with his doctored (*Why am I Famous? What Have I Done? What Am I For?*) versions; Sept 2006.

ISRAEL/ WEST BANK
Balloon Debate,
West Bank Wall.

❸ **Boy with Sand Castle,**
West Bank Wall.

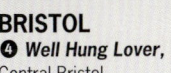

BRISTOL
❹ **Well Hung Lover,**
Central Bristol.

①

GUANTANAMO

"It gives us a very, very bad name, not just internationally."
James A. Barker III, former US Secretary of State, *LA Times*.

The Guantanamo Bay Detention Camp was set up by Secretary of Defense Donald Rumsfeld in 2002 in US Guantanamo Bay Naval Base in Cuba. Banksy created this piece at the height of revulsion at the injustice of US actions from millions around the world, a revulsion he clearly shared.

WHERE IS IT ?
ISLINGTON,
LONDON,
UK.
THE IMAGE HAS SINCE BEEN BUFFED.

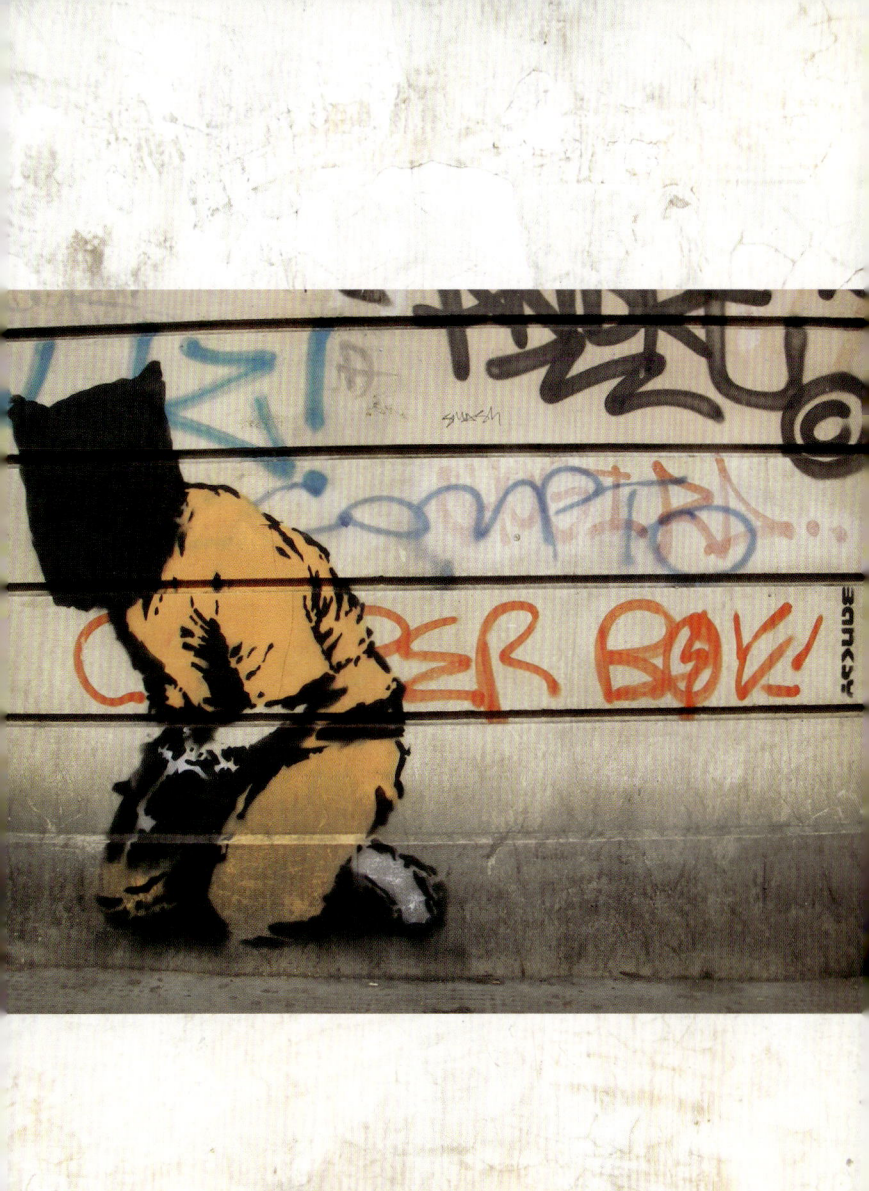

2

SNORTING COPPER

"My main problem with cops is that they do what they're told. They say 'sorry mate, I'm just doing my job' all the fucking time."
Banksy, *Banging Your Head Against a Brick Wall.*

A brilliant situationist piece, mining Banksy's rich vein of policemen caught in compromised situations. The police are some of the prime butts of Banksy's jokes, payback for all those times they hassled and nearly busted him as he stencilled his work.

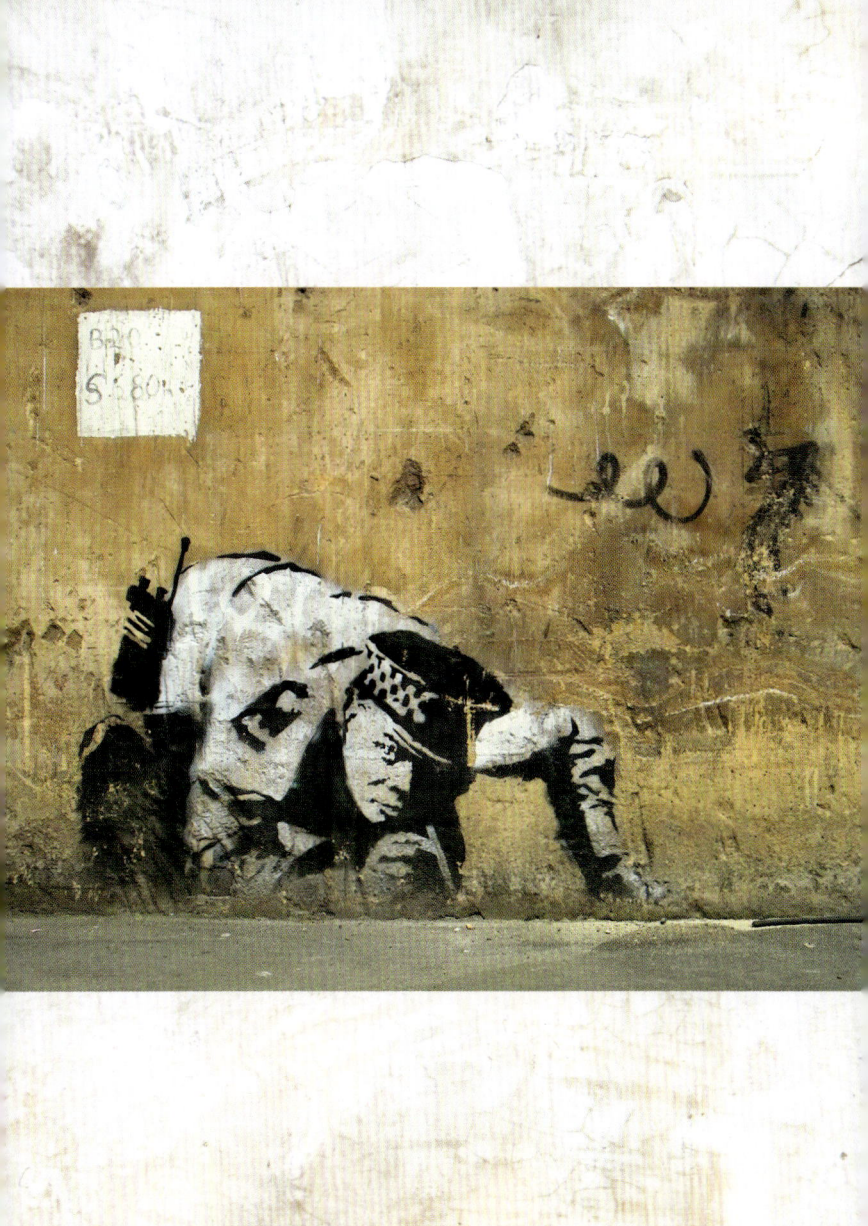

❸

BOY AT THE BEACH

"A wall is a very big weapon. It's one of the nastiest things you can hit someone with."
Banksy, *Banging Your Head Against a Brick Wall*.

All of Banksy's nine images from his 2005 visit to the West Bank, where he highlighted the inhuman nature of the West Bank Wall, live long in the memory. This was one of four where Banksy created an idealised vision of a world where the Wall has been punched in. Against the brutalist concrete we have a scene of sheer optimism and charm. It is saying, how can you allow your children this idyll and yet do nothing about what is happening here?

WHERE IS IT ?
PALESTINIAN SIDE,
WEST BANK WALL,
WEST BANK.

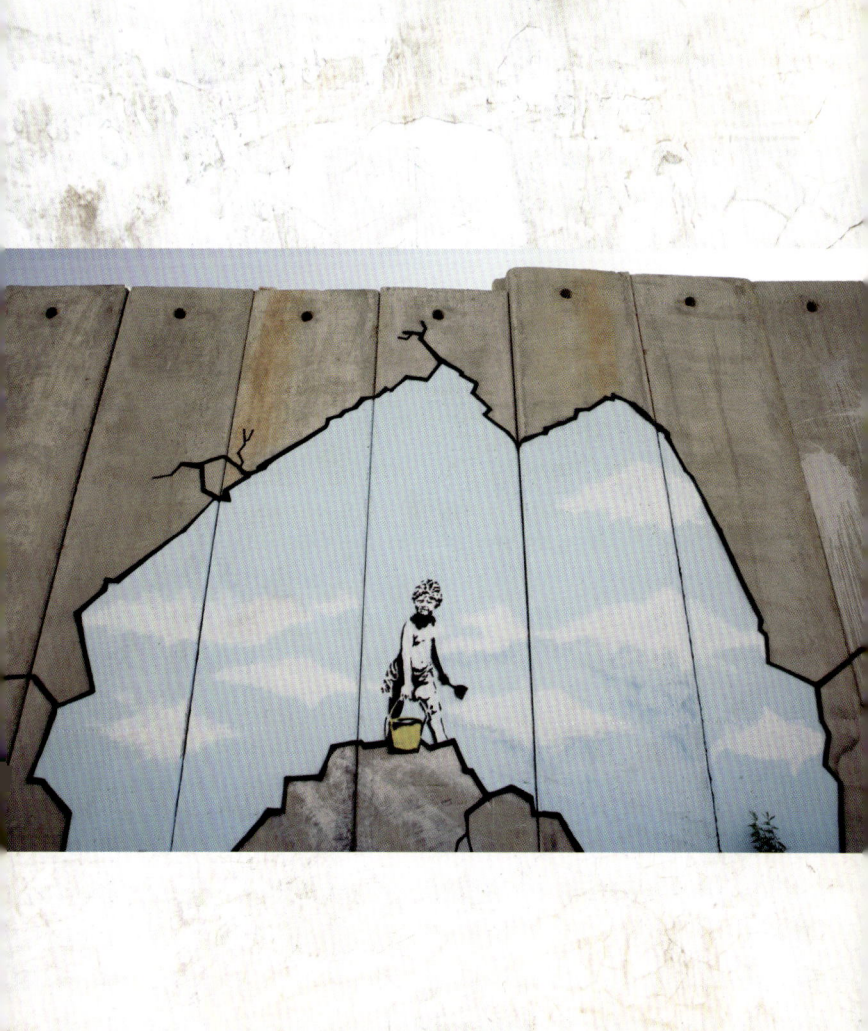

④

WELL HUNG LOVER

"Banksy didn't realise the building contained a sexually transmitted disease clinic."
Manager, STD clinic, Bristol.

A brilliant Banksy in Bristol, with his signature tightly-packed image and word play. The piece appeared on the side of a building housing a clinic for treating sexually transmitted diseases. Just as Banksy loves tweaking the tail of authority figures, so here he is laughing at middle-class, middle-aged respectability.

WHERE IS IT ?
FROGMORE STREET, BRISTOL,
UK.
HAS BEEN PRESERVED.

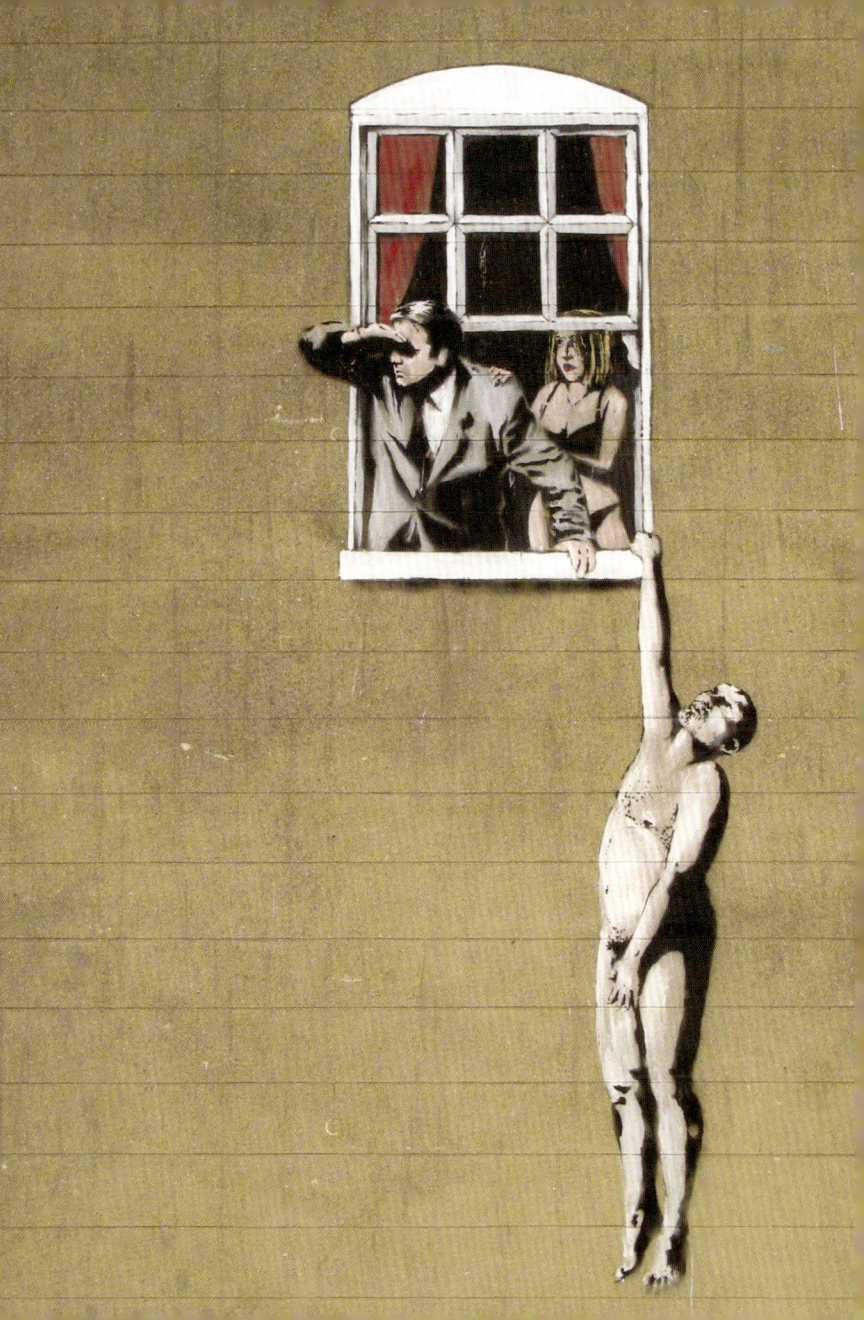

5

SWEEPING IT UNDER THE CARPET

"In the bad old days, it was only popes and princes who had the money for their portraits to be painted."
Banksy on banksy.co.uk

Painted on the side of White Cube Gallery in Hoxton Square, east London, the image ostensibly depicts a maid, Leanne – "a quite feisty lady" – who once cleaned Banksy's room in an L.A. motel. She reappeared in a piece, a defacing of a Damien Hirst spot painting, wittily entitled *Keeping it Spotless*. Auctioned at Sotheby's New York in 2008, the piece sold for an eye-watering $1,700,000, before commission. It remained the highest price achieved by a Banksy for 13 years, until 2019, when Banksy's huge oil, *Devolved Parliament* was sold at Sotheby's, London for £9.9 million ($12.1 million).

WHERE IS IT ?
HOXTON,
LONDON,
UK.
APPEARED ON THE SIDE OF WHITE CUBE GALLERY.
HAS SINCE BEEN BUFFED.

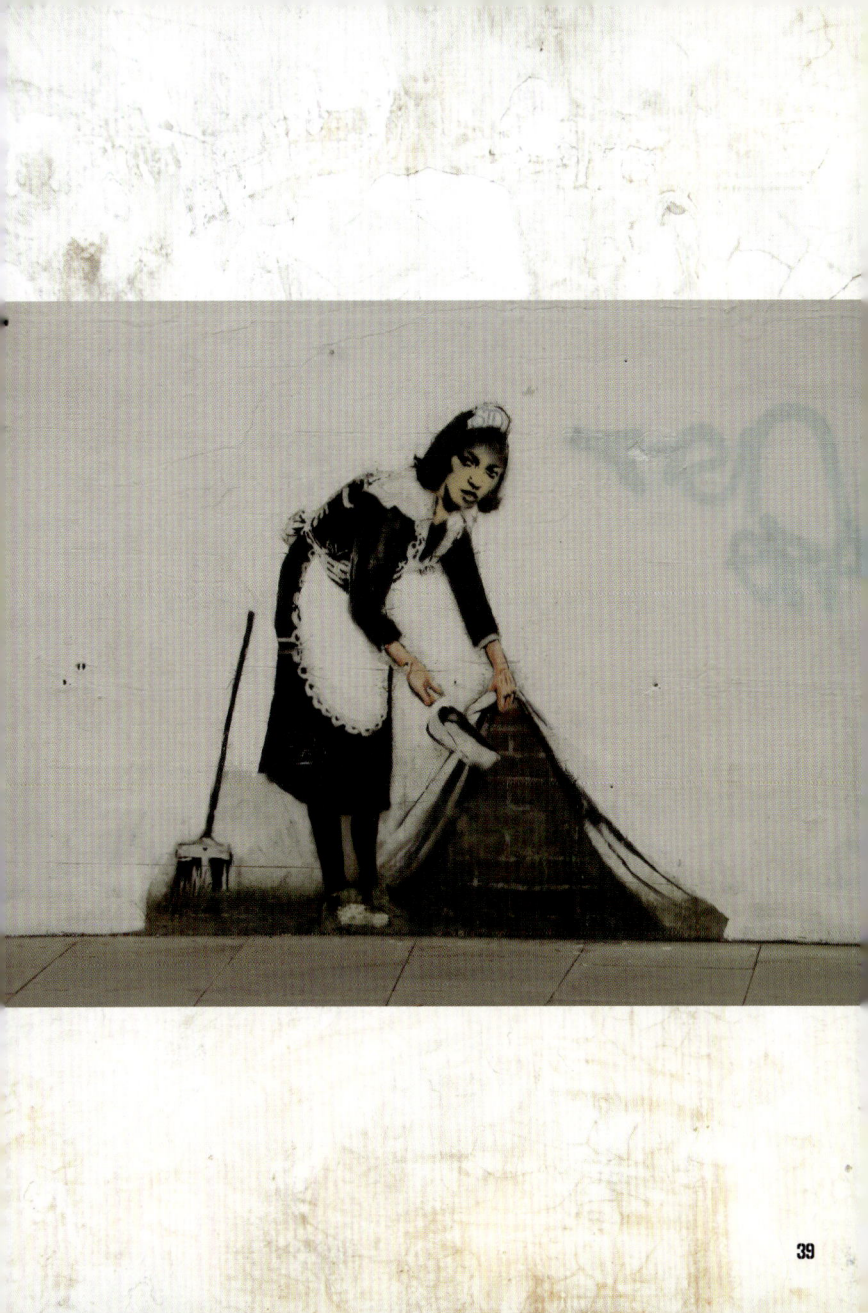

2007–2008

A period of brilliant invention and of hugely successful interventions, particularly the Cans Festival in London. Most striking is his work in London in reaction to the global financial crash, which Banksy is almost prophetic about with his ATM piece. And then there is the very moving and angry work in New Orleans – a searing reaction to Bush's failures in the wake of Hurricane Katrina.

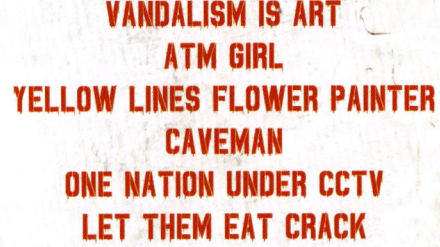

VANDALISM IS ART
ATM GIRL
YELLOW LINES FLOWER PAINTER
CAVEMAN
ONE NATION UNDER CCTV
LET THEM EAT CRACK

BANKSY 2007-2008

Banksy's international travels continue. He's back in Israel, New York and Los Angeles. He creates a new work in Bristol and launches the hugely successful Cans Festival in London. One new location in this period – New Orleans, to investigate and comment on the aftermath of Hurricane Katrina. At a charity auction in Sotheby's, New York, *Keeping it Spotless* achieves a world record (for a Banksy) of $1.9 million dollars.

EXHIBITIONS AND INTERVENTIONS

NEW YORK
Sotheby's New York charity auction (for Aids in Africa). *Keeping it Spotless* sells for $1.9m; February 2008.

The Village Pet Store and Charcoal Grill, Banksy's first official exhibition in NYC; 5th Oct 2008.

LONDON
Bonhams Auctioneers, London. *Space Girl Bird* auctioned for £288,000 ($403,200); 27th April 2008.

Cans Festival, Leake Street, Waterloo station. 3rd–5th May 2008.

NEW YORK
❻ *Let them Eat Crack,* Bowery.

LOS ANGELES
You Looked Better on Myspace, Beverly Hills.

❹ *Caveman* Beverly Hills.

Flower Aerial Girl, Hollywood.

Flower Girl Hollywood.

NEW ORLEANS
Nola Girl with Umbrella.

Abe Lincoln.

Looting National Guards.

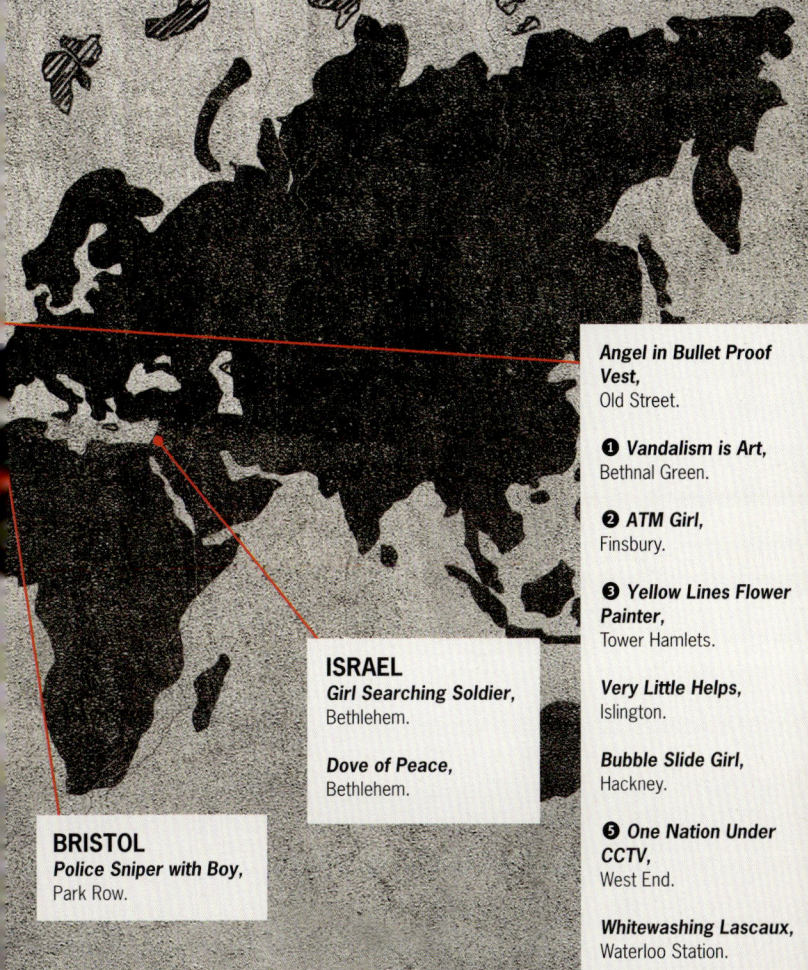

Angel in Bullet Proof Vest,
Old Street.

❶ *Vandalism is Art,*
Bethnal Green.

❷ *ATM Girl,*
Finsbury.

❸ *Yellow Lines Flower Painter,*
Tower Hamlets.

Very Little Helps,
Islington.

Bubble Slide Girl,
Hackney.

❺ *One Nation Under CCTV,*
West End.

Whitewashing Lascaux,
Waterloo Station.

ISRAEL
Girl Searching Soldier,
Bethlehem.

Dove of Peace,
Bethlehem.

BRISTOL
Police Sniper with Boy,
Park Row.

1

VANDALISM IS ART

"All artists are willing to suffer for their work. But why are so few prepared to learn to draw? " **Banksy**

This is Banksy once more operating on a number of levels. The simple fact is that street art *is* vandalism, except when it's art, and then again sometimes it's both. This just-pubescent cock is the simplest, most stupid, form of graffiti. By placing his witty artist daubing his inspired oils, Banksy transforms it into art, and it lives up to its title.

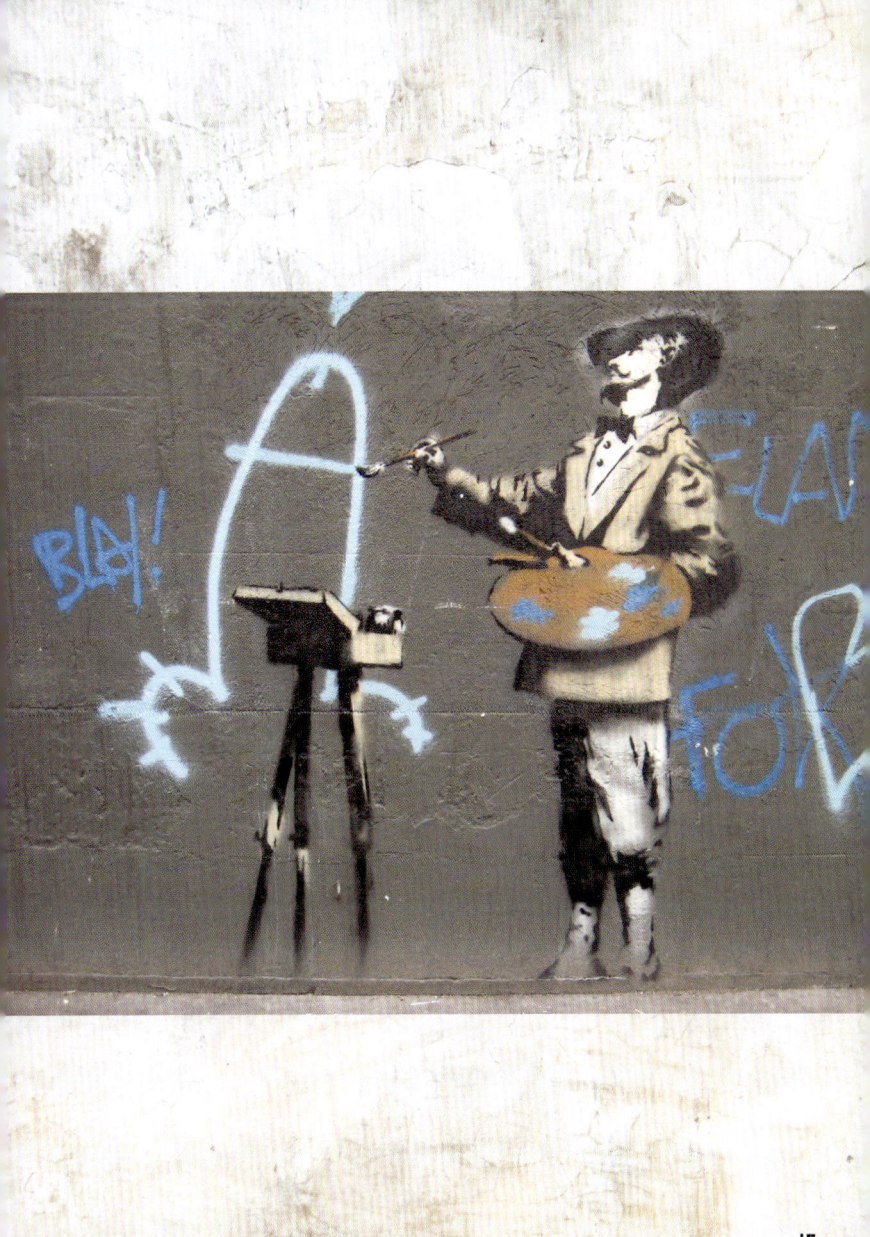

②

ATM GIRL

"Cost of the global financial crash of 2007-08: $2,800,000,000,000 (2.8 trillion dollars)."
The Guardian, quoting a Bank of England report in 2008.

This was created in 2007, a few months before the biggest financial crash since the 1930s, when the world's most 'respectable' banks were shown to be the most corrupt, from selling sub-prime mortgage securities (even when they knew they were worthless) as AAA stock, to mis-selling payment protection insurance (which has to date cost the banks $55 billion in fines).

WHERE IS IT ?
EXMOUTH MARKET,
FINSBURY,
LONDON,
UK.

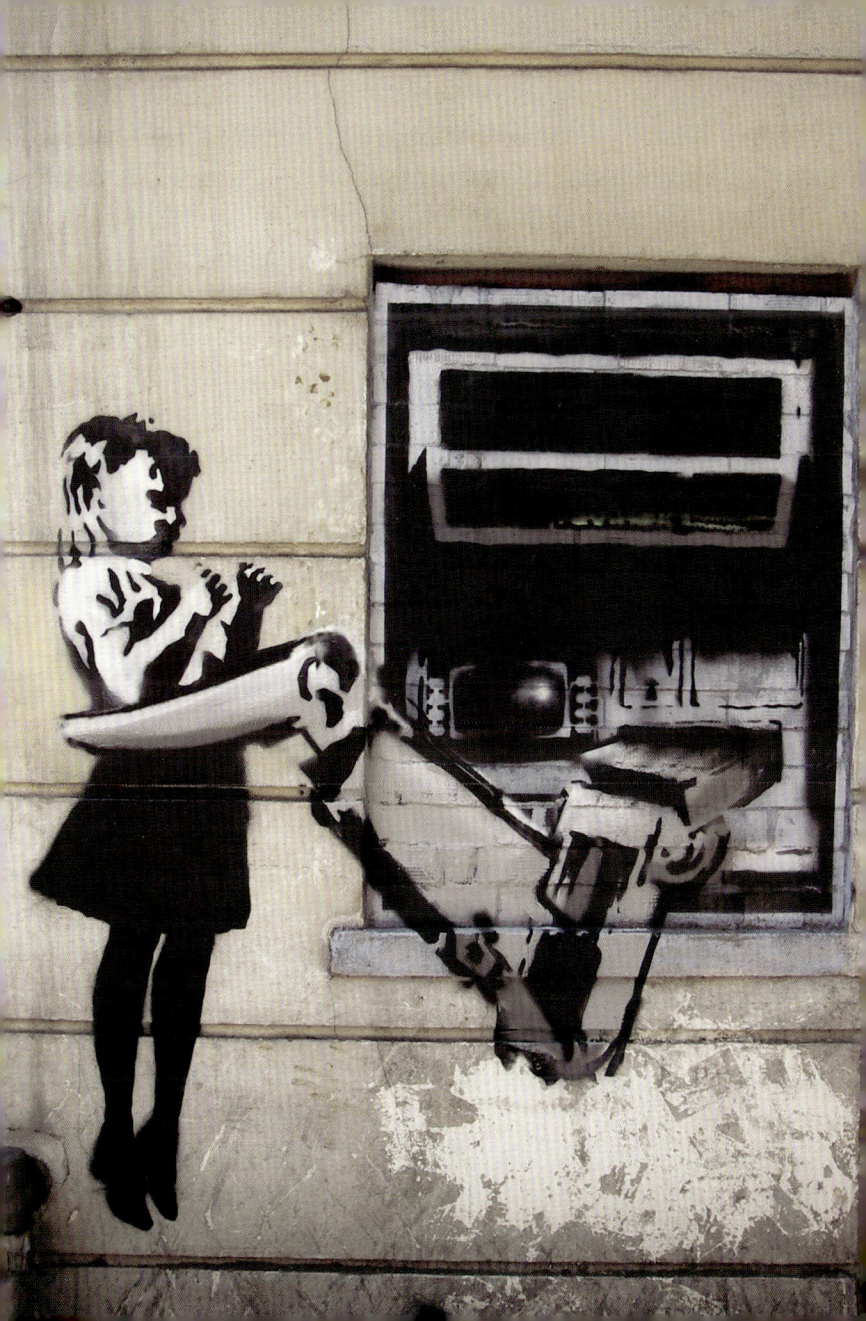

❸

YELLOW LINES FLOWER PAINTER

"A lot of people never use their initiative because no one told them to."
Banksy.

Double yellow parking lines indicate no parking at any time on UK streets. Banksy shows the painter 'artist' is having a well-earned rest; it is no accident that he painted this on the side of a working men's social club. Always awake to bureaucratic cliché, Banksy usurps the over-use of self-congratulatory logos by local authorities, with a stencil of Tower Hamlets borough council supposedly 'claiming' authorship.

WHERE IS IT ?
BETHNAL GREEN,
LONDON,
UK.
LINES ON PAVEMENT BUFFED BY LOCAL COUNCIL.
ONLY THE FLOWER ON THE WALL REMAINS.

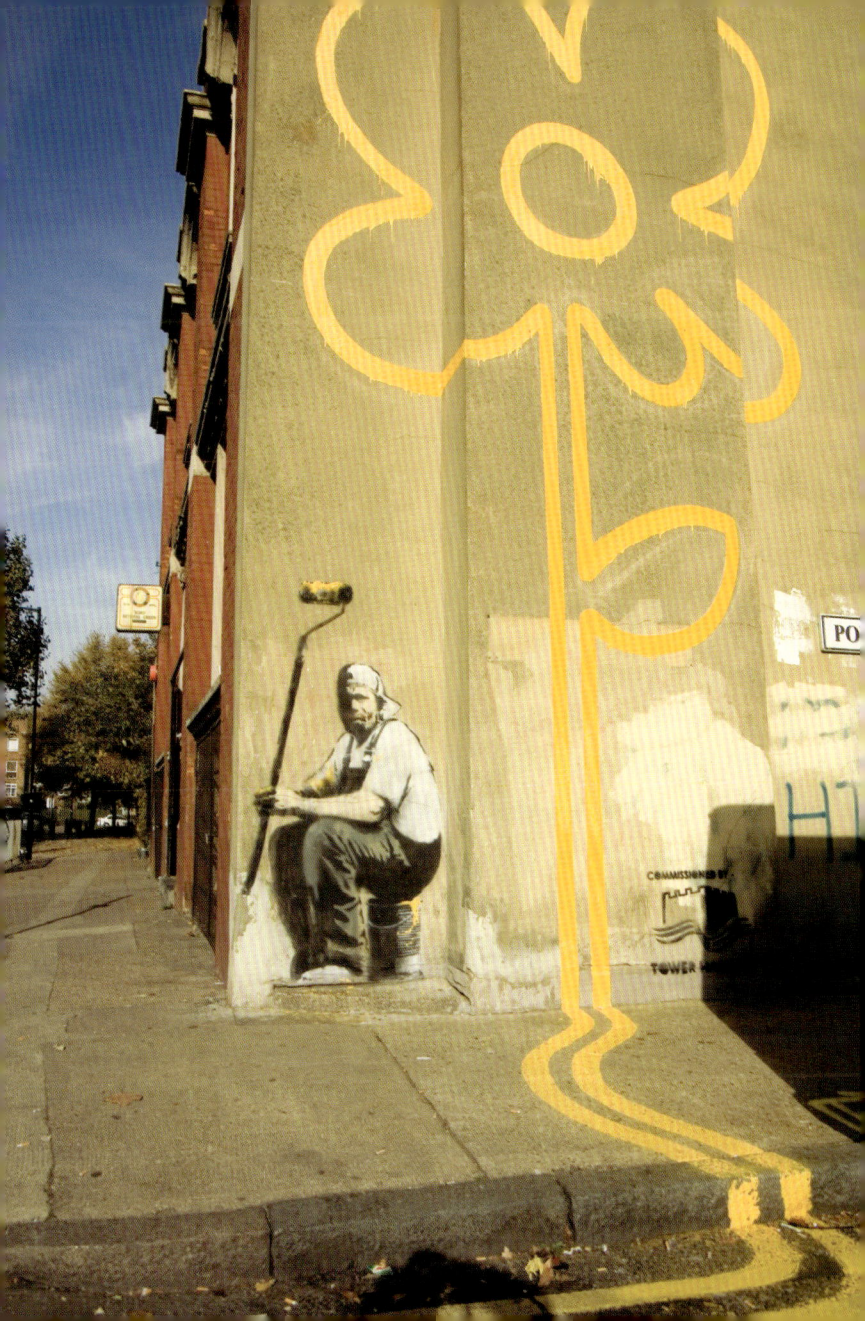

4

CAVEMAN

"The holy grail is to spend less time making the picture than it takes people to look at it." **Banksy.**

The start of Stanley Kubrick's *2001 A Space Odyssey* has that unforgettable opening scene, where an ape throws a femur into the air which spins into space and morphs into a rotating nuclear satellite in outer space. Bansksy's caveman hasn't thrown the bone, he's holding onto it almost as though evolution has been arrested. In his other hand he has a tray of fast food. This is modern man, still just a caveman feeding his primeval appetite.

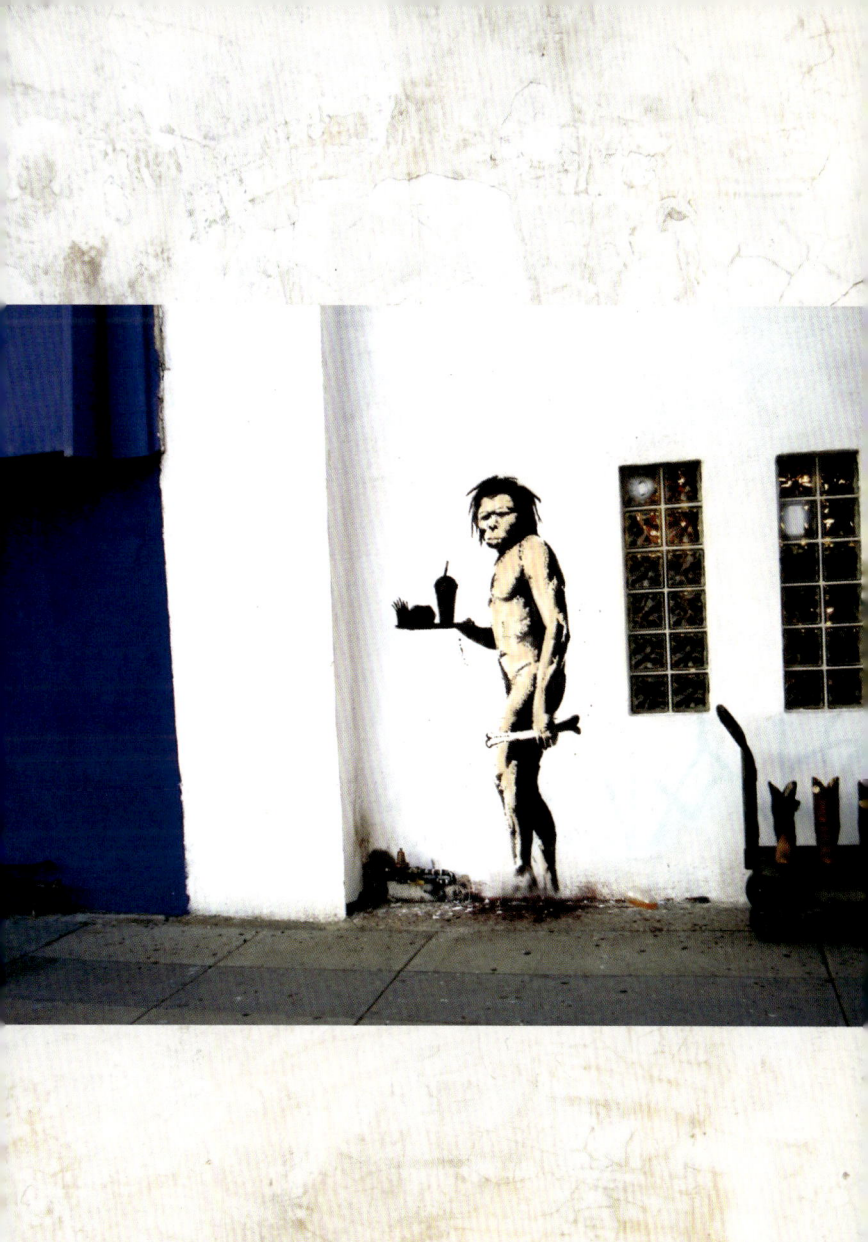

5

ONE NATION UNDER CCTV

"One nation under God."
US Pledge of Allegiance.

"I pledge allegiance to the flag of the United States of America, and to the Republic for which it stands, one Nation, under God, indivisible, with liberty and justice for all." So runs the USA's Pledge of Allegiance. This has everything we love in a Banksy. A brilliant twist to language, and visual wit in spades. It was painted in a secure area belonging to the Post Office, a few feet from a security camera, highlighting the fact that the UK is the most surveilled country on the planet.

WHERE IS IT ?
NORTH OF OXFORD STREET,
LONDON,
UK.
NO LONGER THERE;
WESTMINSTER CITY COUNCIL
ORDERED ITS REMOVAL.

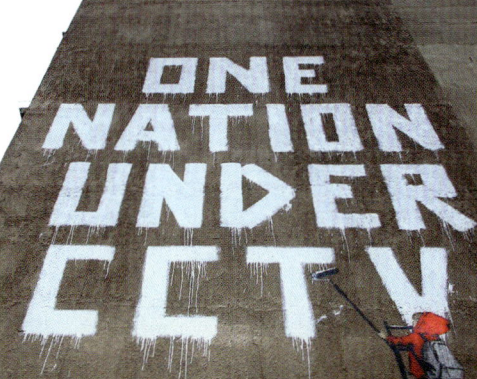

6

LET THEM EAT CRACK

"Let them eat cake."
Unfairly attributed to Marie Antoinette in 1788.

The reference to the Marie Antoinette mis-quote, catches just the right spirit of contempt the bankers felt for regular Americans in 2008, who were having their mortgages foreclosed, whose houses were collapsing in value, together with, in so many instances, their life savings. "You having trouble coping with that?" he seems to be saying, "well, there's always crack."

WHERE IS IT ?
SOHO,
NEW YORK,
USA.
PAINTED OVER BY NOVEMBER 2008.

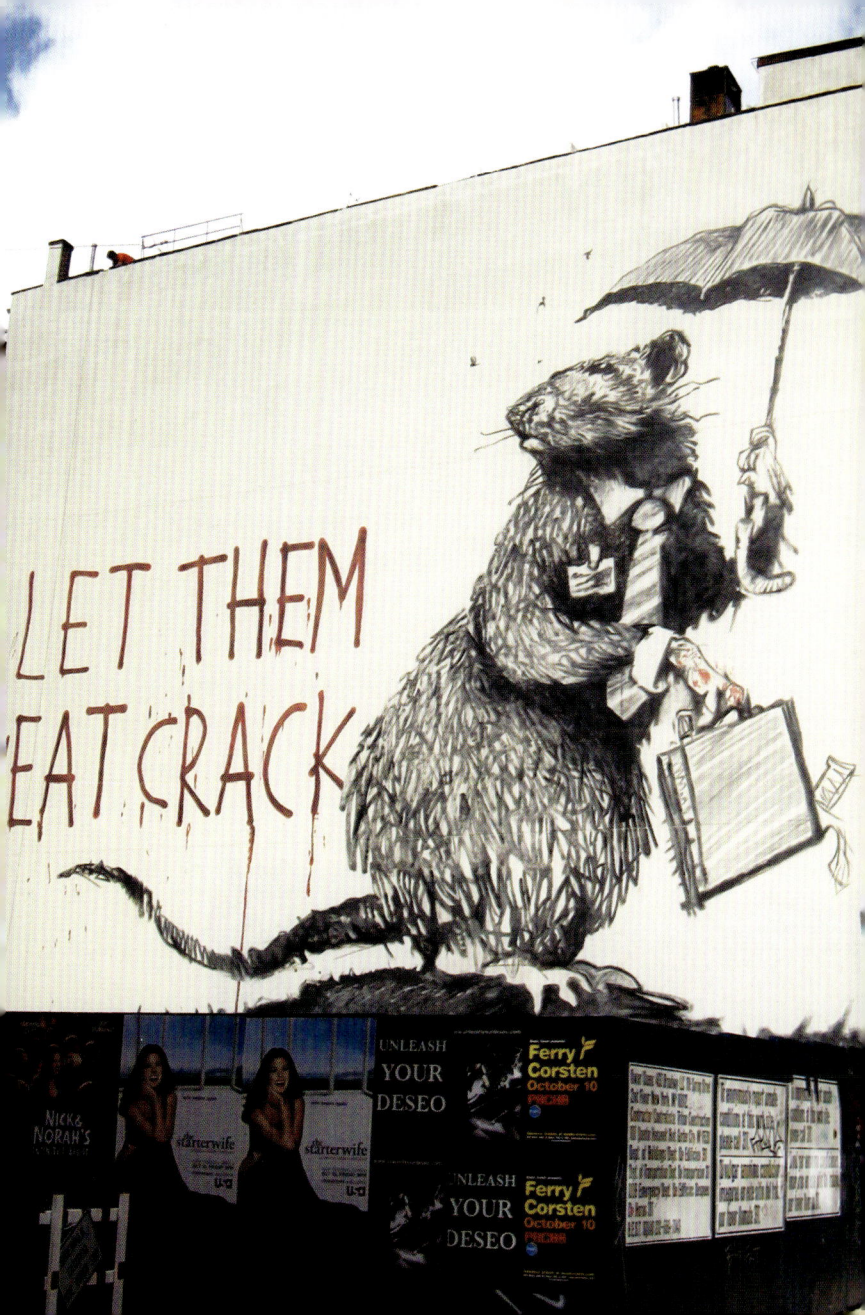

2009-2010

A brilliantly productive period, with the reach
of street art taken to new heights with his
documentary *Exit Through the Gift Shop*, nominated
for the Best Documentary Oscar.
Banksy produces brilliant work in L.A., New York
and Detroit. He is again ahead of the game with his
criticism of Obama's drone assassination strategy,
with *Airstrike*; Obama's popularity does not stop
Banksy's searching eye seeing what is really going
on in US foreign policy.

NO FISHING
EXIT THROUGH THE GIFT SHOP
GUARD ON DUTY
PARK
TESCO SAND CASTLE
CALL AN AIRSTRIKE
I LOVE NY

BANKSY 2009-2010

Banksy undertakes a lot of international travel in support of *Exit Through The Gift Shop*. First the launch at the Sundance Film Festival in Utah, then Boston, Toronto, New York and L.A., followed by San Francisco, with a segway to Detroit.

Otherwise it was London again and a seaside trip down to Hastings on the English south coast, for another dig at supermarket giant, Tesco.

EXHIBITIONS AND INTERVENTIONS

BRISTOL
Banksy Vs Bristol Museum,
Bristol City Museum, June 2009.

❷ UTAH
World premiere of *Exit Through the Gift Shop*, Sundance Film Festival, Park City; 24th January 2010.

DETROIT
Detroit Tree,
in an abandoned Packard Car Plant.

NEW YORK
Will Work for Idiots,
Manhattan.

Wheatpaster,
Chinatown.

Liberty,
Long Island City.

❼ I Love NY,
Lower Manhattan.

LOS ANGELES
❸ Guard on Duty,
La Brea and 4th.

❹ Park,
Broadway, Downtown.

SAN FRANCISCO
❻ Airstrike,
Chinatown.

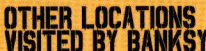

OTHER LOCATIONS VISITED BY BANKSY

MALI
January, 2009

BOSTON
May, 2010

TORONTO
May, 2010

DUNGENESS
August, 2010

HASTINGS
❺ Tesco Sand Castle,
Beach front.

LONDON
Last Graffiti Before Motorway,
North Circular Road.

Boombox Boy,
Dalston.

❶ No Fishing,
Camden.

Rollerhead Heron,
Camden Lock.

1

NO FISHING

"We are concerned that Banksy's street art glorifies what is essentially vandalism."
Diane Shakespeare, official with the
***Keep Britain Tidy* campaign.**

Banksy is here returning to one of his tropes: pointing out the petty signage which is the mark of the quietly oppressive state. Here the boy has fished out a sign banning fishing. Someone has thrown it in the canal, thus removing the restriction. Even in this dank corner of London, Banksy seems to be saying, you are under surveillance.

WHERE IS IT ?
REGENT'S CANAL,
CAMDEN,
LONDON,
UK.

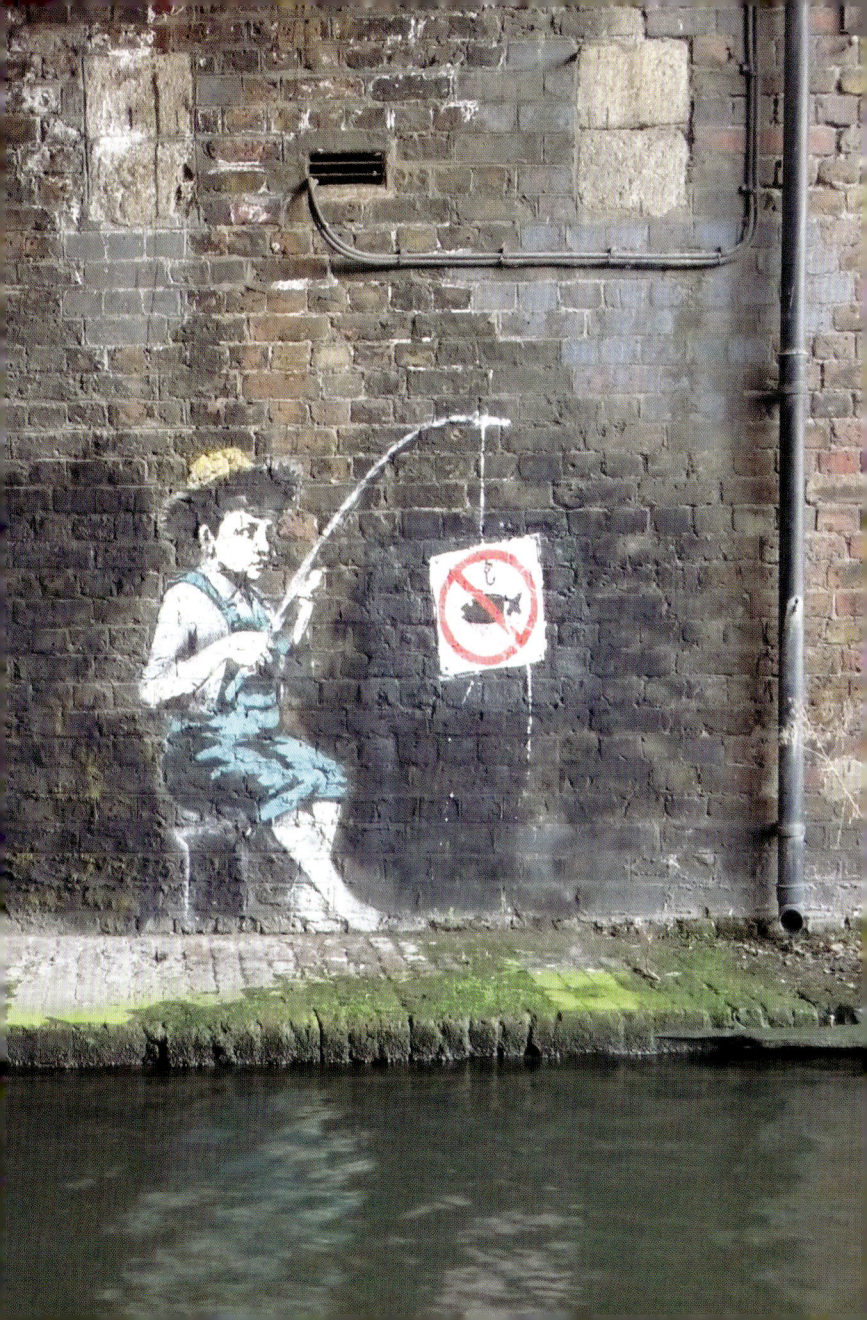

❷

EXIT THROUGH THE GIFT SHOP

**"Exit *could be a new subgenre:
the prankumentary."*
*The New York Times.***

The poster for Banksy's brilliantly clever *Exit Through the Gift Shop* movie was a triumph, showing art as just another consumer good. In brilliant juxtaposition we see a homeless man, shopping trolley full of black bin bags, walking the streets (a kind of gift shop, given the art on show), about to take the Mona Lisa to the checkout – the last man one would see in a gallery shop. And that's the point. Gallery art isn't about art, it's just another form of middle class consumption.

WHERE IS IT ?
MOVIE SHOWN AT THE LOS ANGELES
THEATER, ARTS DISTRICT,
L.A.,
USA.

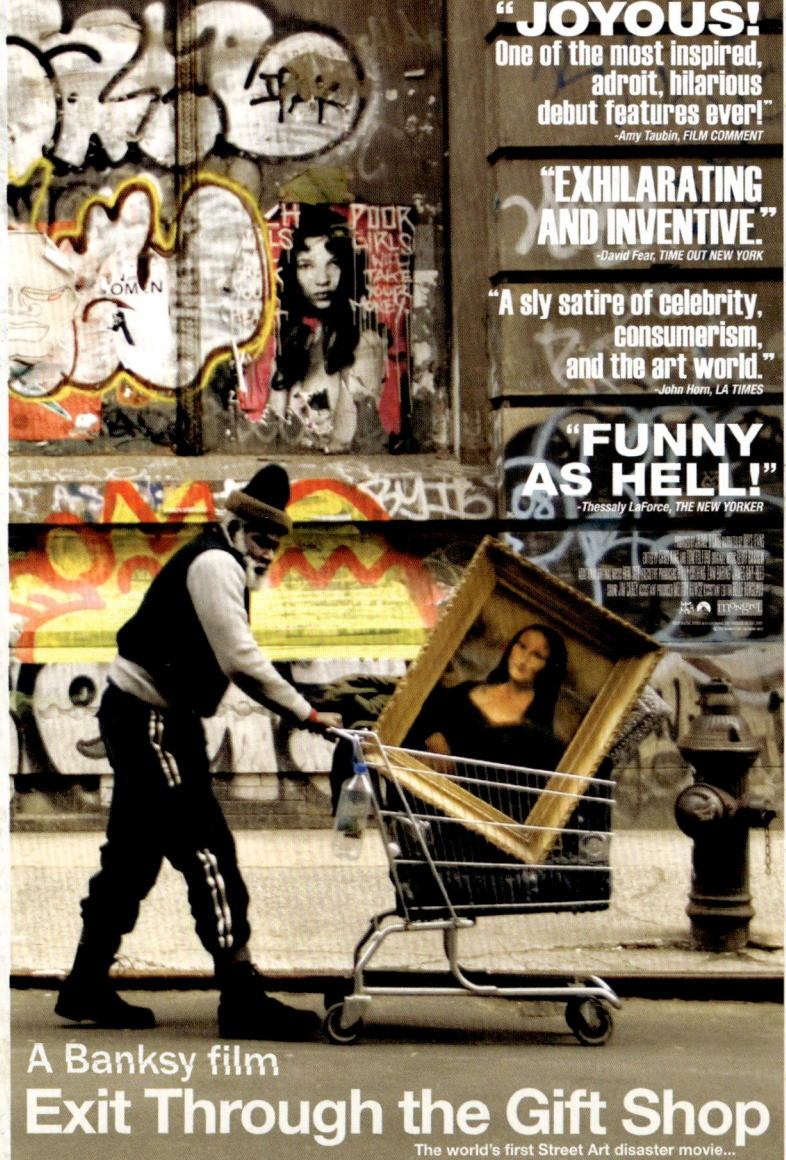

3

GUARD ON DUTY

"US private security spending is estimated to rise to $68 billion annually by 2019."
Freedonia Group report.

Banksy effortlessly sends up the U.S. security industry with his serious, butch security guard, and his emasculating pink balloon dog. The dog has a touch of Jeff Koons about it and is depicted with a leaping stance. However the leash is limp and he is muzzled. It's one of Banksy's most satisfying works.

WHERE IS IT ?
LA BREA AND 4TH,
LOS ANGELES,
USA.
REMOVED A FEW DAYS AFTER IT WENT UP.
WHEREABOUTS UNKNOWN.

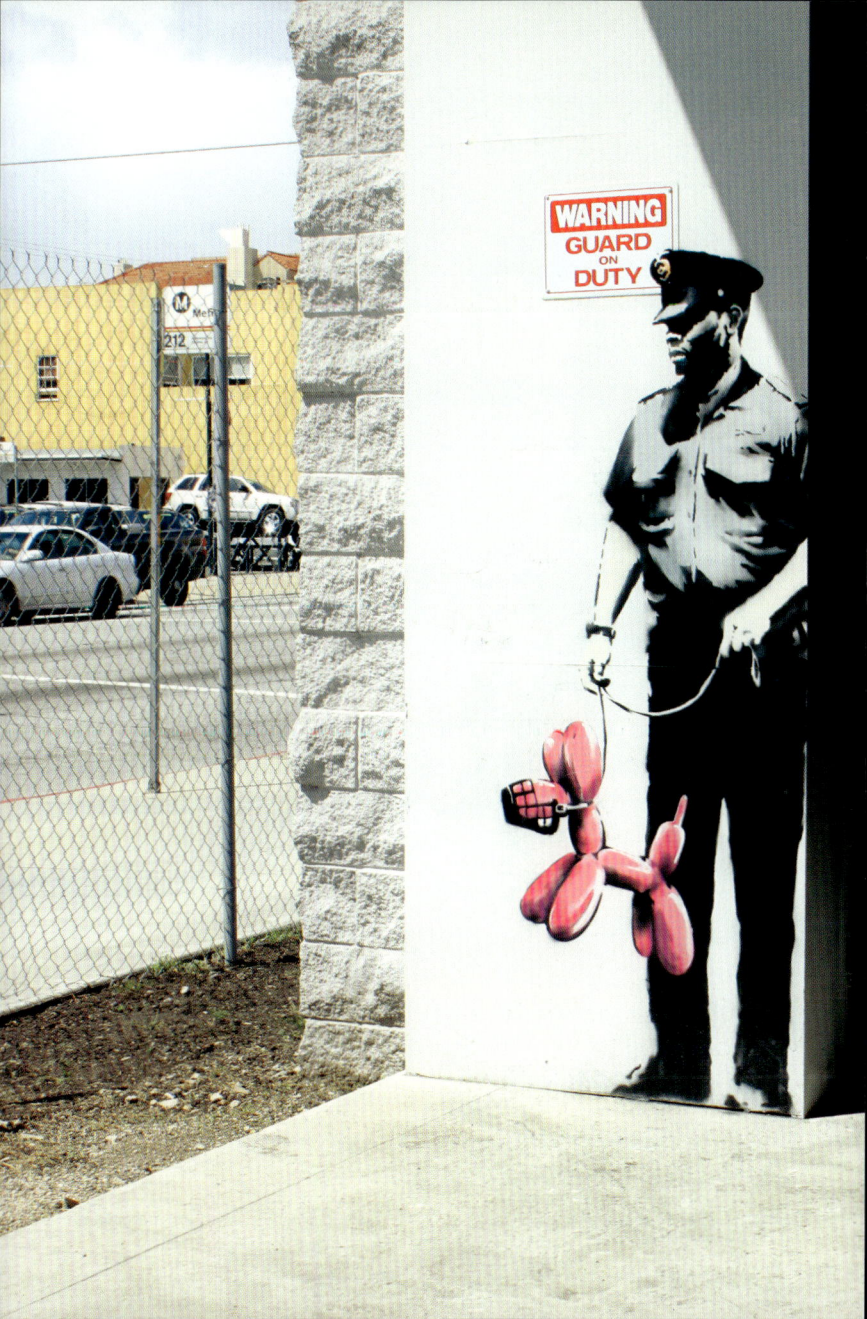

④
PARK

"Good artists copy, great artists steal."
Pablo Picasso.

In broad terms, Banksy is here criticising our addiction to the automobile, an apposite statement in L.A., which, as cities go, is the ultimate car junky. The traditionally-dressed little girl on the swing, the top loops cleverly passed through the crossbar of the 'A', is wonderfully conceived. It's an admonishment to society and to adult selfishness: how come it's so easy to find car parking, so hard to create a park?

WHERE IS IT ?
BROADWAY,
DOWNTOWN,
LOS ANGELES,
USA.

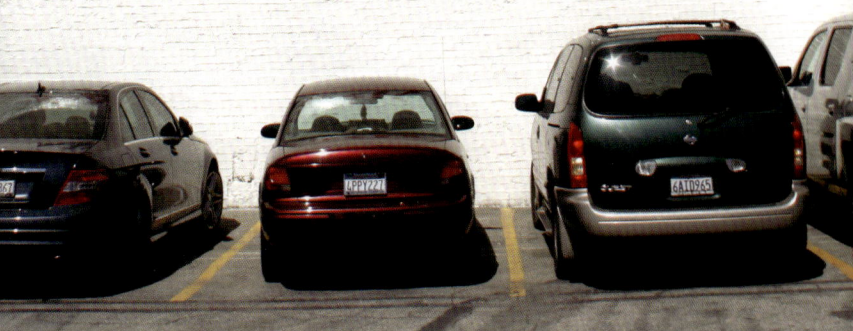

5

TESCO SAND CASTLE

*"We have a zero tolerance policy on graffiti and that is absolutely right...
I have agreed that Banksy can be an exception to our rule and can stay."*
Councillor Jay Kramer, Hastings Borough Council.

The British supermarket mega chain, Tesco, has been a major target for criticism from Banksy. Tesco in particular has faced major opposition from some communities over its plans to build new mega-stores in out-of-town centres. The castle, with its little Union Jack, represents Britain. The word 'Tesco' has been pricked into the sand on each turret. The boy, we suspect, signifies the Tesco corporate machine, aiming at constant capitalist expansion.

WHERE IS IT ?
BEACH FRONT,
HASTINGS,
UK.

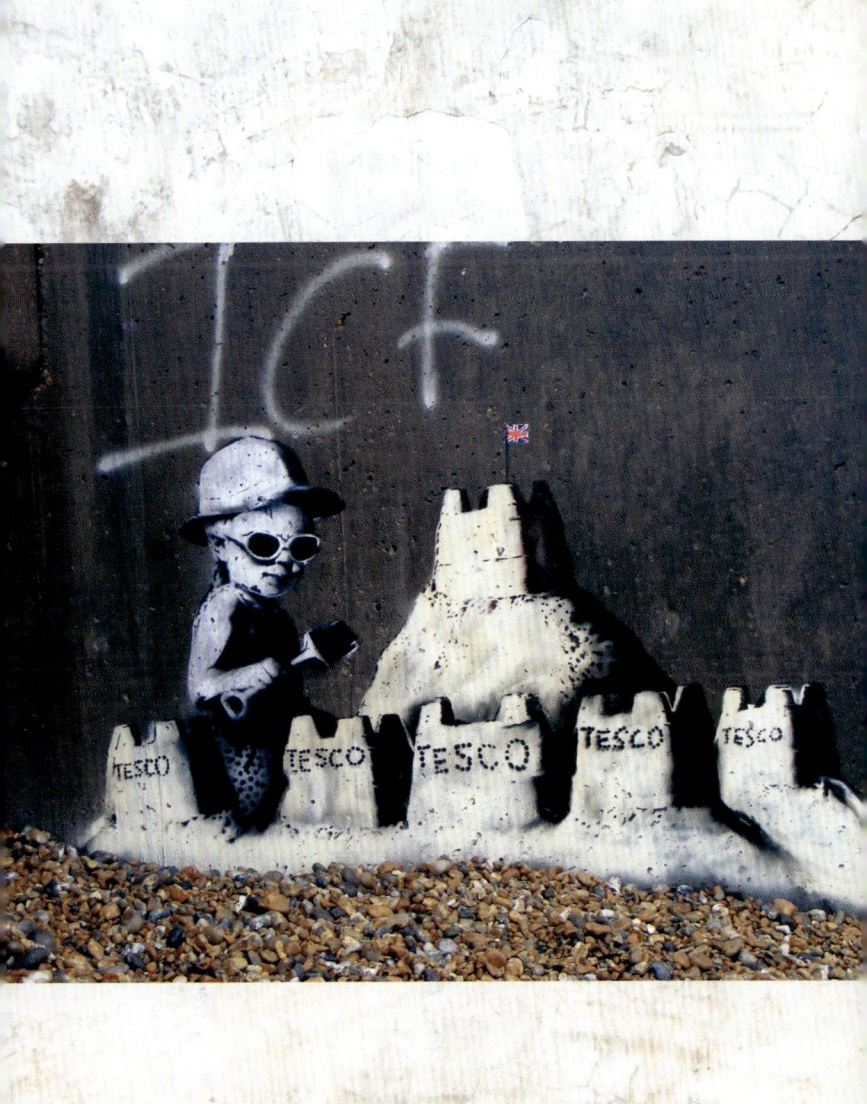

6

CALL AN AIRSTRIKE

"We must define our effort not as a boundless 'Global War on Terror', but rather as a series of persistent, targeted efforts to dismantle specific networks of violent extremists."
President Barack Obama, 2010.

In 2010, Barack Obama was in office with a commitment to end the US wars in Iraq and Afghanistan, an admission the Bush administration's ground troop invasions had failed. The flip side of troop reductions was, however, a major increase in US air strikes, particularly from drone attacks. This shows Banksy at his most politically prescient.

WHERE IS IT ?
CHINATOWN,
SAN FRANCISCO,
USA.

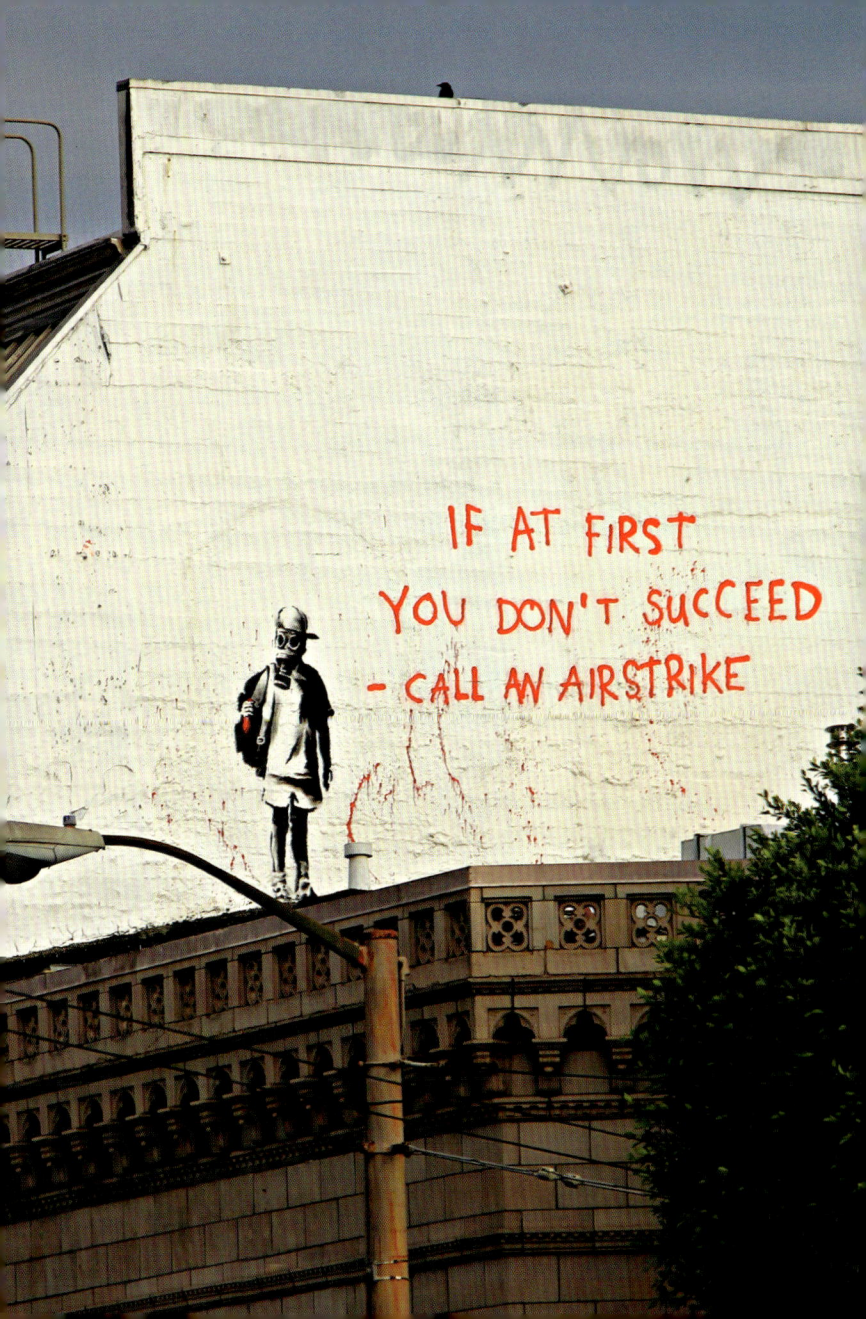

7

I LOVE NY

> *"No one is a bigger supporter of the arts than I am...defacing somebody's property... is not my definition of art. Or it may be art, but it should not be permitted."*
> **New York Mayor Michael Bloomberg.**

A development of a similar piece created earlier the same year in San Francisco, this has all the qualities of juxtaposition, anachronism, mocking of common cliché and subliminal irony which define a classic Banksy. It's location – on Cedar Street, just above Wall Street – gives a possible interpretation. Wall Street, and by extension NYC is, after the appalling 2008 financial crash, as sick as ever, carrying on recklessly just as before.

WHERE IS IT ?
LOWER MANHATTAN,
NYC,
USA.

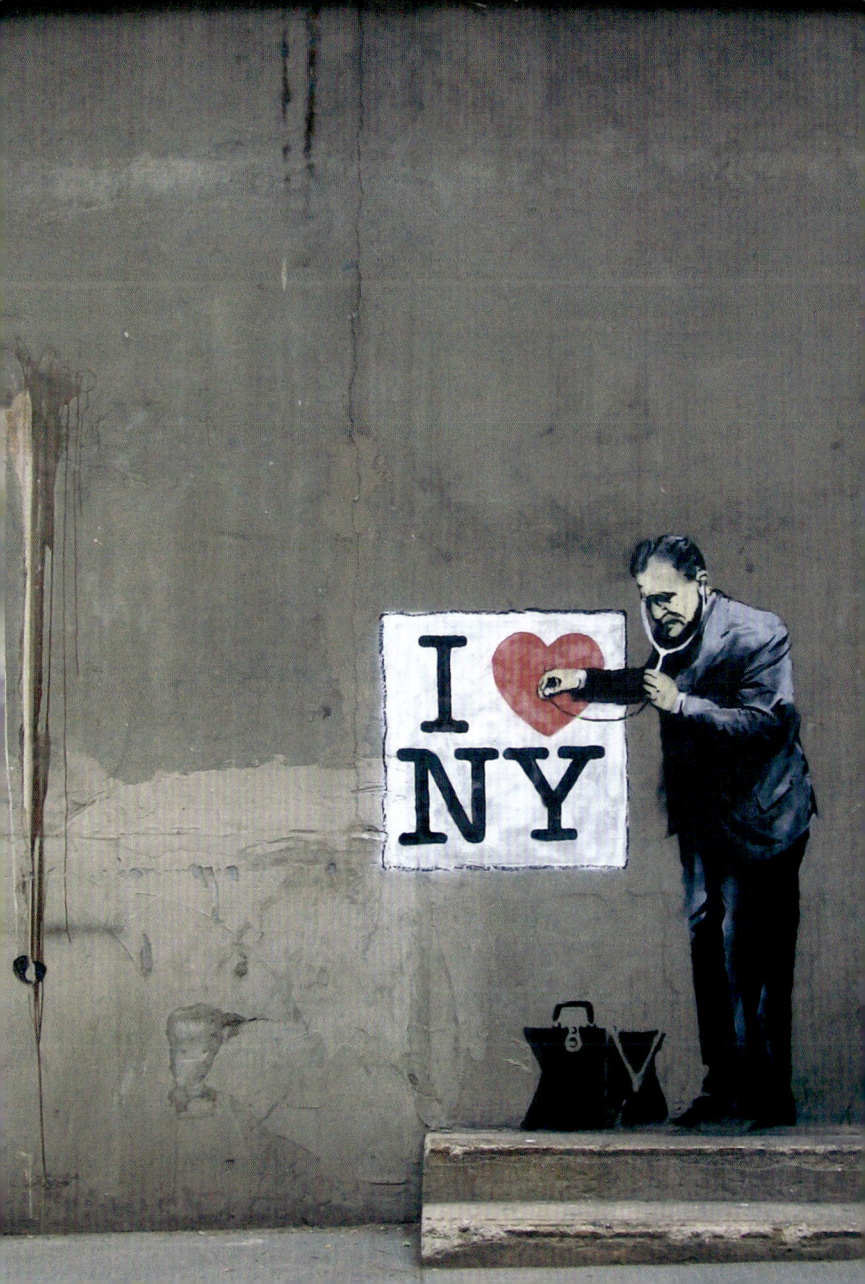

2011-2012

Great work in London and L.A. dominates this period. In L.A. side-swipes at the Disney Corporation. Back in London the humbug around the Queen's Jubilee celebrations inspires the anti-child labour piece outside a north London Poundland. Banksy returns to themes of the global financial crash and its austerity aftermath.

CHARLIE BROWN FIRESTARTER
CRAYOLA SHOOTER
SLAVE LABOUR
THE LIFESTYLE YOU ORDERED IS CURRENTLY OUT OF STOCK

BANKSY 2011-2012

In this period new works in the US are limited to Los Angeles. Banksy does create some fantastic new pieces in London, focussing on child labour, migration, consumerism and post-crash economic austerity. A number of these end up being sold in the US.

Banksy also takes what is beginning to look like a habitual trip to the English south coast, this time to Lyme Regis, where he creates his somewhat whimsical *Origami Crane*.

LOS ANGELES
❶ *Charlie Brown Firestarter*,
Beverly Hills.

❷ *Crayola Shooter*,
Westwood.

Drunk Mickey,
Sunset Strip.

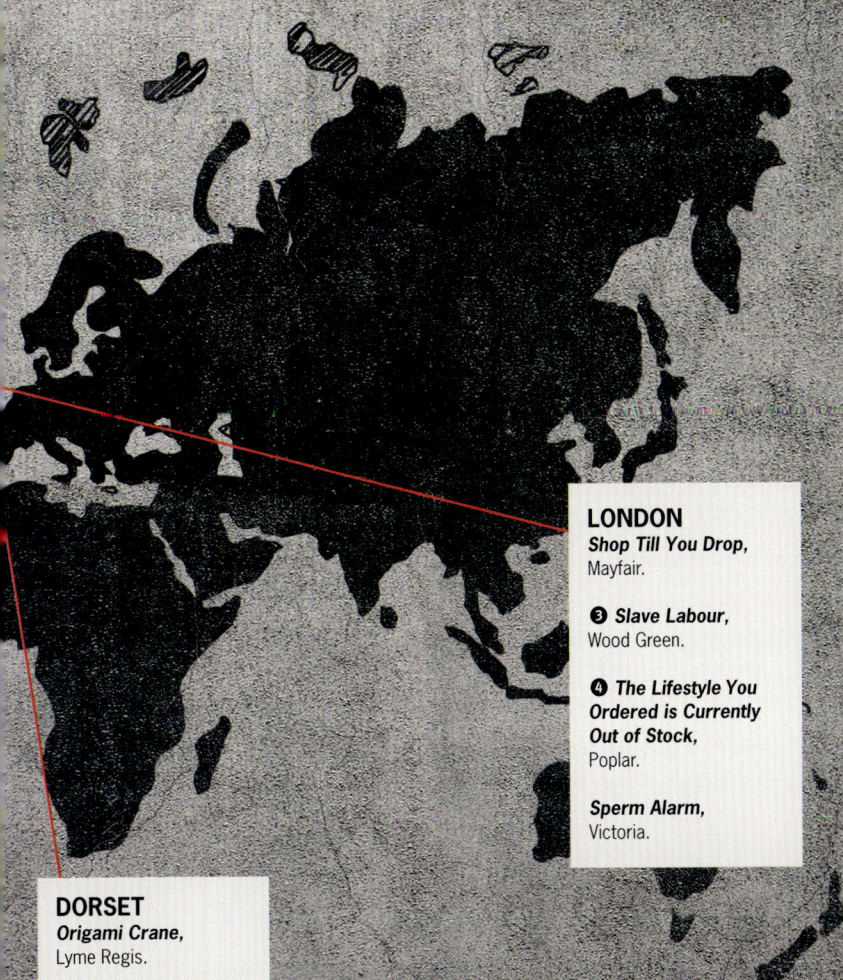

LONDON
Shop Till You Drop,
Mayfair.

❸ *Slave Labour,*
Wood Green.

❹ *The Lifestyle You Ordered is Currently Out of Stock,*
Poplar.

Sperm Alarm,
Victoria.

DORSET
Origami Crane,
Lyme Regis.

1

CHARLIE BROWN FIRESTARTER

"What's the good of living if you don't try a few things?"
Charles M. Schulz, *The Complete Peanuts*, 1959-1960.

This hilarious image of Charlie Brown, the *Peanuts* cartoon character who, in a way, defines the all-American kid, is shown petrol can in hand, fag in mouth, about to commit arson. The piece was stencilled on the side of a fire-damaged building in Beverly Hills.

WHERE IS IT ?
BEVERLEY HILLS,
LOS ANGELES,
USA.
WAS REMOVED SHORTLY AFTER
THE STENCIL APPEARED.
WHEREABOUTS UNKNOWN.

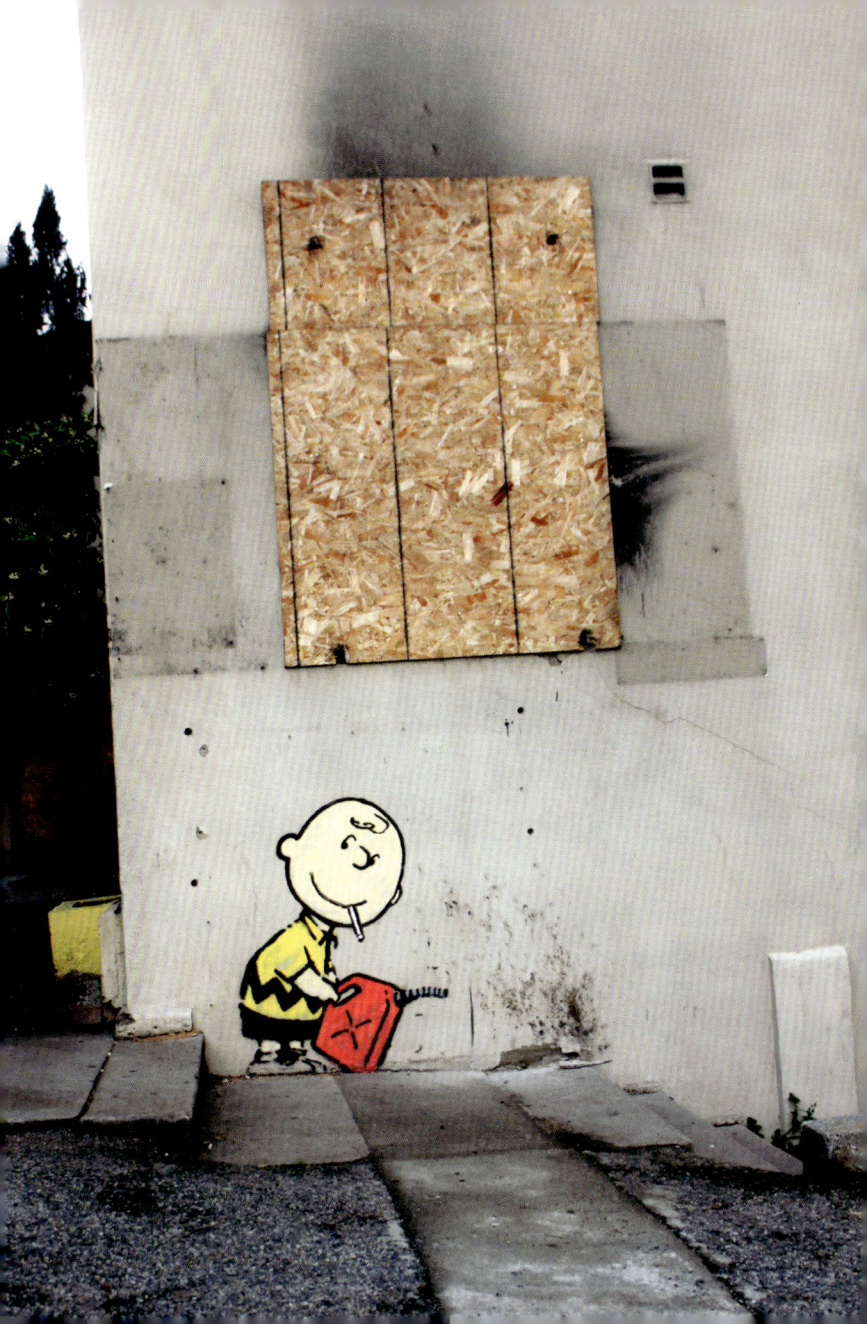

2

CRAYOLA SHOOTER

"There are an estimated 250,000 child soldiers in the world today."
War Child Charity.

Another Banksy taking a pop, literally, at petty local authority restrictive signage. This also reminds us of one of those pictures of VietCong kids from the Vietnam war in the '60s. The piece could also be a reference to kids getting ensnared and brutalised in wars in the developing world, or, closer to home, L.A. gangland kids getting into gun crime too young.

WHERE IS IT ?
WESTWOOD,
LOS ANGELES,
USA.
BUFFED SHORTLY AFTER IT APPEARED.

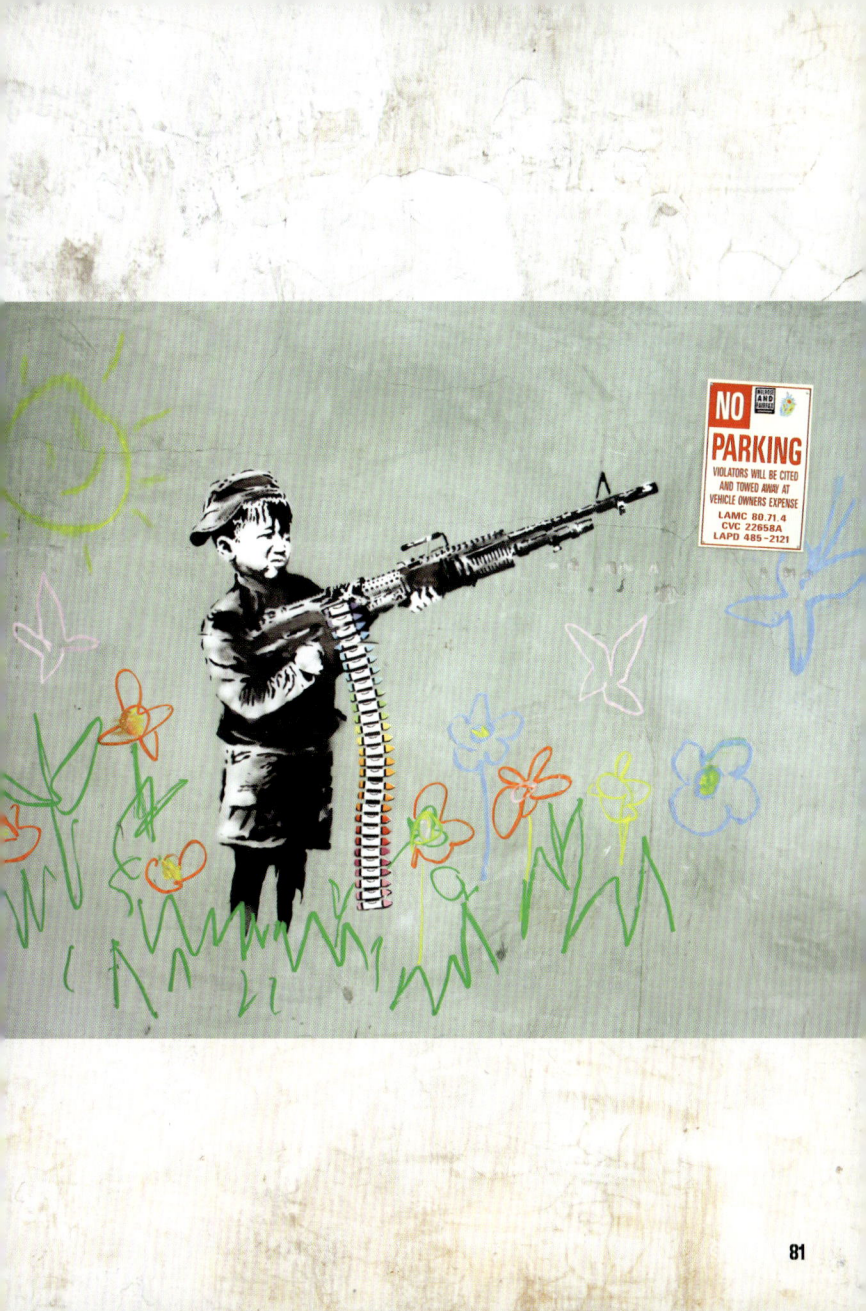

❸

SLAVE LABOUR

"You have deprived a community of an asset that was given to us for free... I call you, and your consciences, to pull the piece from both potential sales and return it to its rightful place."
Wood Green MP Lynne Featherstone.

2012 was the year of both the Queen's Jubilee and of the London Olympics. This piece, painted on the side of a tacky Poundland shop in the north London suburb of Wood Green, shows Banksy enjoying a pop at the royals and all the schmalz culture around patriotism. In the midst of all the tat produced to celebrate 60 years of feudal monarchial rule, have the British paused to think why their Union Jacking bunting is so cheap? The piece was later auctioned for $1.1 million.

WHERE IS IT ?
WOOD GREEN,
LONDON.
WAS 'REMOVED' AND EVENTUALLY SOLD AT
AUCTION IN
LONDON. A REPLICA, NOT QUITE EXACT, IS NOW
UNDER PERSPEX IN THE ORIGINAL LOCATION.

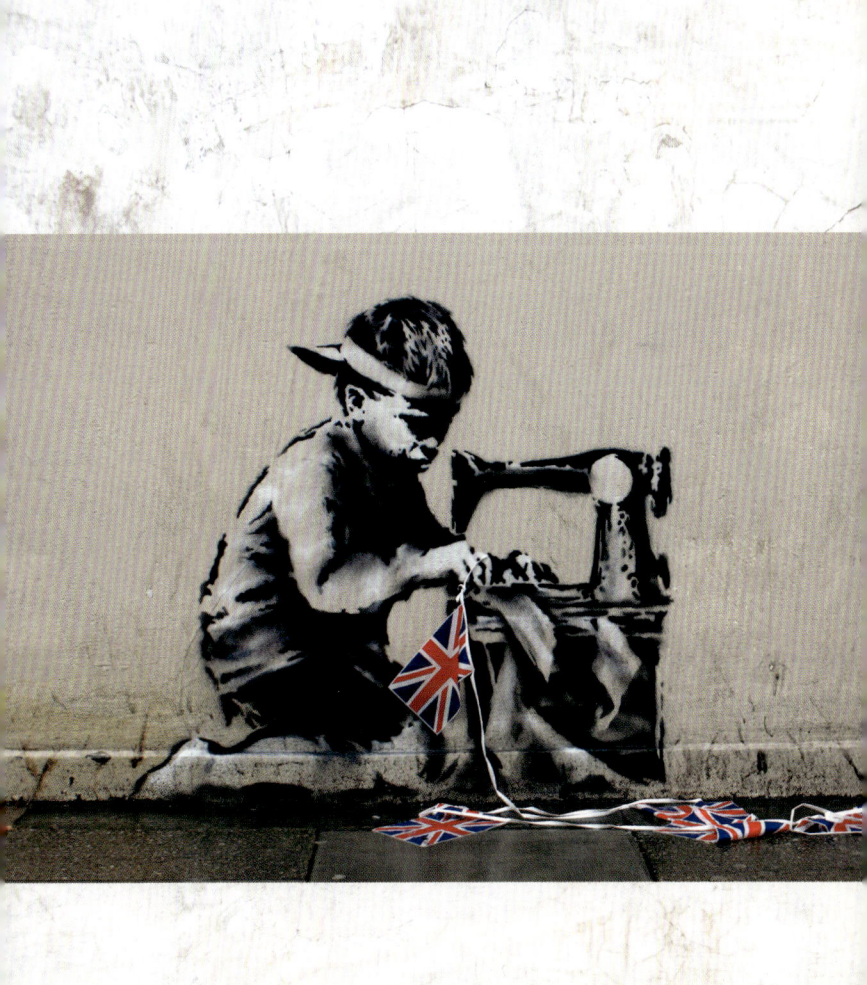

❹

THE LIFESTYLE YOU ORDERED IS CURRENTLY OUT OF STOCK

"We're all in this together."
George Osborne, UK Chancellor of the Exchequer.

The location of the piece in Poplar, an area with many residents on benefits, is somewhat ironic, and takes the anti-consumerist surface meaning of the piece onto another level. For many locals, there was never a question of buying into a lifestyle. In this context, 'lifestyle' means just about getting by, due to the UK government's austerity policies. Austerity, yup you guessed it, to pay for the debts of the bankers in the skyscrapers, whose lifestyle, of course, remains very much in stock.

WHERE IS IT ?
POPLAR,
LONDON,
UK.

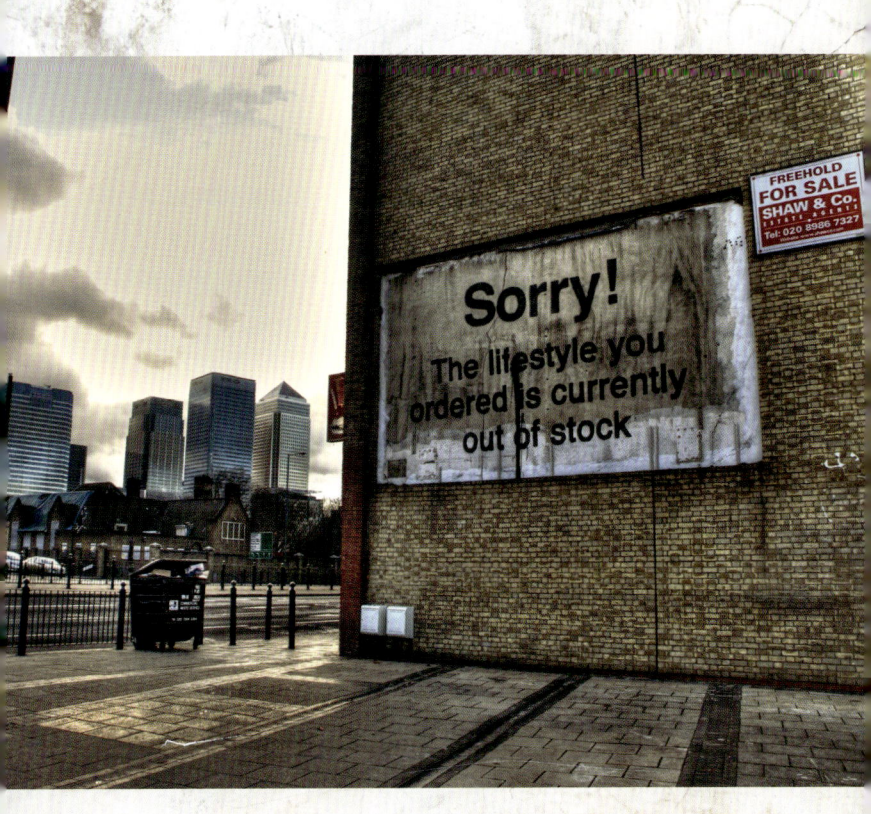

2013

The year of the triumph of the New York residency. 31 days, and 30 works around the city revealing again high wit and visual eloquence outstripping, by far, any other street artist. Themes include individual freedom, the evils of Nazism, animal cruelty, overbearing corporate power (this time McDonald's) and a risky tribute to 9/11. His anti-war *Crazy Horses* raises the bar – Banksy's most searing anti-war piece to date.

THE STREET IS IN PLAY
GHETTO 4 LIFE
WAITING IN VAIN
JAPANESE SCENE
SHOE SHINE
SIRENS OF THE LAMBS
ETERNITY
OS GEMEOS COLLABORATION

BANKSY 2013

The year of the brilliant New York 'residency', entitled *Better Out Than In*. Most works were created in mid and lower Manhattan – Soho, Hell's Kitchen and the East and West Villages. However Banksy also ventured to the smart Upper West Side, did his stall in Central Park and created works in The Bronx, Queens, Brooklyn and Staten Island. Some of the installations were on trucks, which drove all over Manhattan. The Day 16 piece also moved to various McDonald's around the city.

Day 1:
The Street is in Play, Allen Street, Lower East Side.
Day 2:
This is My New York Accent, Allen Street, 11th Ave and 25th St.
Day 3:
You Complete Me, 6th Ave and 24th St.
Day 4:
Occupy, The Musical; Dirty Underwear, The Musical; Playground Mob, The Musical. Lower East Side, Williamsburg and Bushwick.
Day 5:
3-D Mobile Waterfall; mobile garden (includes rainbow, waterfall and butterflies) created in delivery truck.
East Village and various locations throughout the city during the residency.
Day 6:
Rebel Rocket Attack, Video, showing Dumbo shot down by Syrian rebels, posted on Banksy's YouTube channel.
Day 7:
Battle to Survive a Broken Heart, Van Brunt St & King St, Red Hook, Brooklyn.
Day 8:
I Have a Theory That You Can Make Any Sentence Seem Profound by Writing the Name of a Dead Philosopher at the End of it. Plato. 255 Freeman St, Greenpoint.
Day 9:
Crazy Horses, 159 Ludlow St, Lower East Side.
Day 10:
Beaver With No Parking Sign, 274 Bradford St, East NYC.

Day 11:
Sirens of the Lambs, stuffed animals in a slaughterhouse truck.
Started in the Meatpacking District, then toured the city for two weeks.
Day 12:
Concrete Confessional, Cooper Square & East 7th St, East Village.
Day 13:
Spray Art for Sale. Banksy sells authenticated works for $60 a pop at a stall in Central Park.
Day 14:
What We Do in Life Echoes in Eterni..., 69th St & 38th Ave., Queens.
Day 15:
Twin Towers Tribute, Jay St & Staple St, Tribeca.
Day 16:
Ronald McDonald Shoe Shine, 839 Westchester Ave., South Bronx and various other McDonald's locations.
Day 17:
Japanese Footbridge Scene, Graham Ave & Cook St, Bed Stuy.
Day 18:
Banksy x OSGEMEOS Open Air Gallery, W 24th St, under the Highline.
Day 19:
Vaginal Anthill, Staten Island.
Day 20:
Boy With Hammer, Upper West Side.
Day 21:
Ghetto 4 Life, Elton Avenue and 153rd St, South Bronx.

Day 22:
Everything but the Kitchen Sphinx, 127th St & 35th Ave.
Day 23:
Today's art has been cancelled due to police activity.
Message on Banksy's Instagram page. Rumours of his arrest proved unfounded.
Day 24:
Waiting in Vain, Larry Flynt's Hustler Club, West Side Highway, Hell's Kitchen.
Day 25:
Grim Reaper in a Bumper Car, E Houston St & Elizabeth St.
Day 26:
The Grumpier You Are, the More Assholes You Meet, Message on back of truck which departed from Sunset Park.
Day 27:
This Site Contains Blocked Messages, Banksy's response to the *New York Times* rejecting his op-ed column. It was published instead on Banksy's website.
Day 28:
Tagging Robot, Coney Island.
Day 29:
The Banality of the Banality of Evil, Housing Works thrift shop, 23rd St.
Day 30:
Bronx Zoo Leopard, Yankee Stadium.
Day 31:
Inflatable Throw-Up, Banksy tagged his name in inflatable bubble writing on the last day of his residency.
Borden Ave & 35th St, Queens.

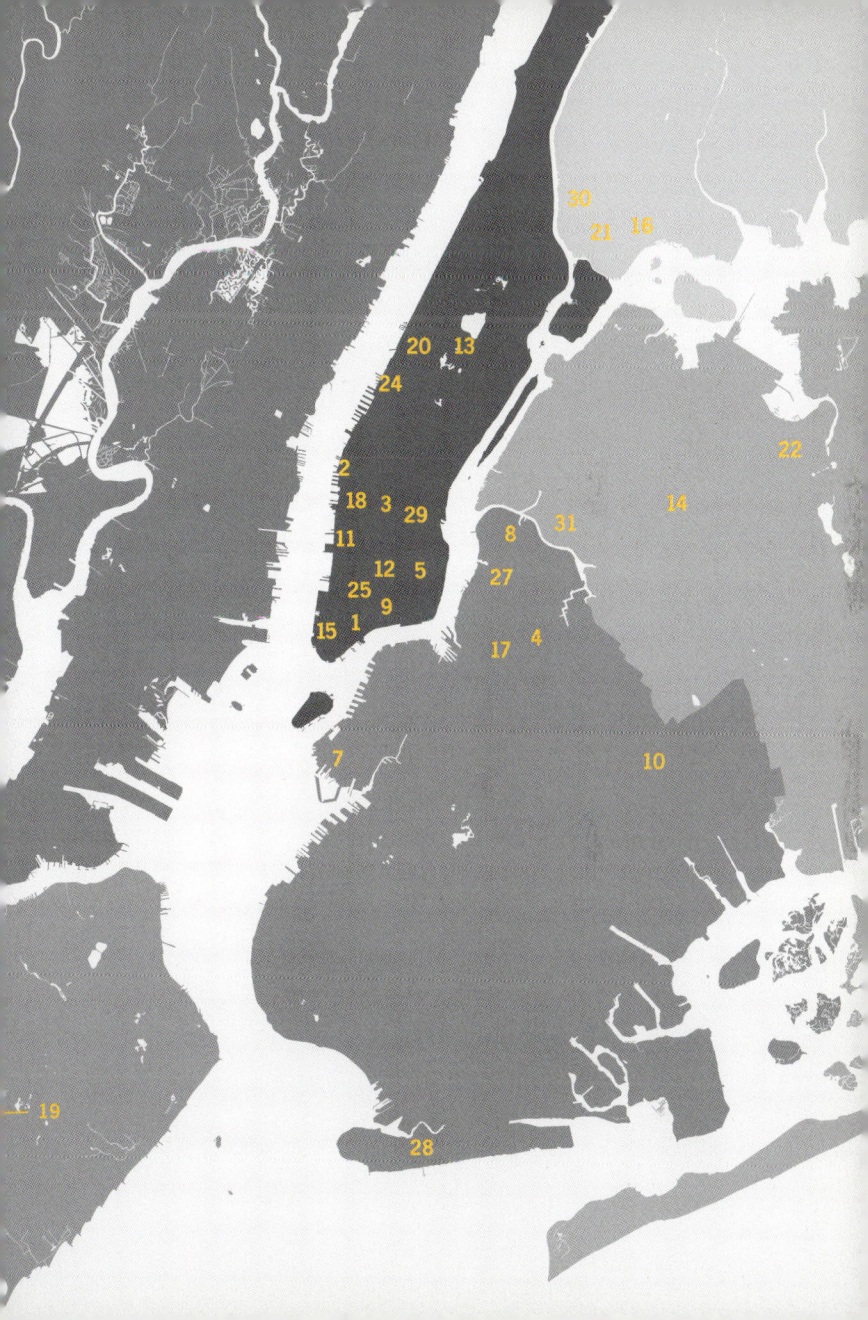

1

THE STREET IS IN PLAY

*"People say graffiti is ugly,
irresponsible and childish...
but that's only if it's done properly."*
Banksy.

Also known as *Graffiti is a Crime,* this was Banksy's first work for his month-long New York residency. It is a charming comment on the anti-establishment yet young nature of street art, but also of the camaraderie and team effort often involved in getting illicit art onto walls.

WHERE IS IT ?
LOWER EAST SIDE,
NYC,
USA.
BUFFED WITHIN 24 HOURS.

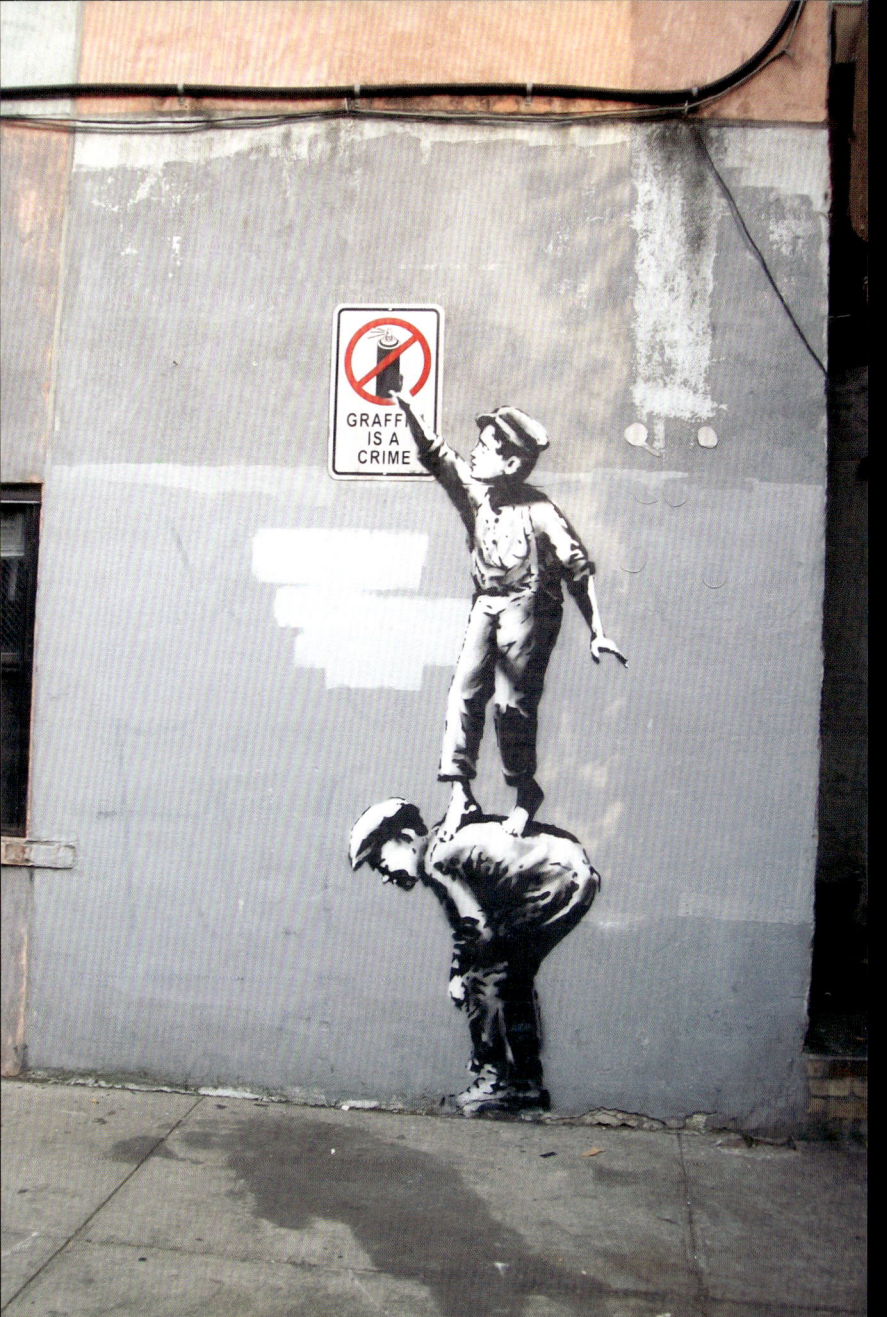

2

GHETTO 4 LIFE

"Many Bronxites are upset at Banksy's choice of words, and they are right to be upset."
Ruben Diaz Jr., President Bronx Borough.

A wonderfully provocative piece, which elicited just the right sort of righteous indignation. This is in fact such a witty send-up of the white adopters of graffiti culture, toffs who like to make out they're from the street. Perhaps Banksy is even sending himself up a little here. In that sense it is an homage, a desire that street culture will not be anaesthetised and cleaned up.

WHERE IS IT ?
BRONX,
NYC,
USA.

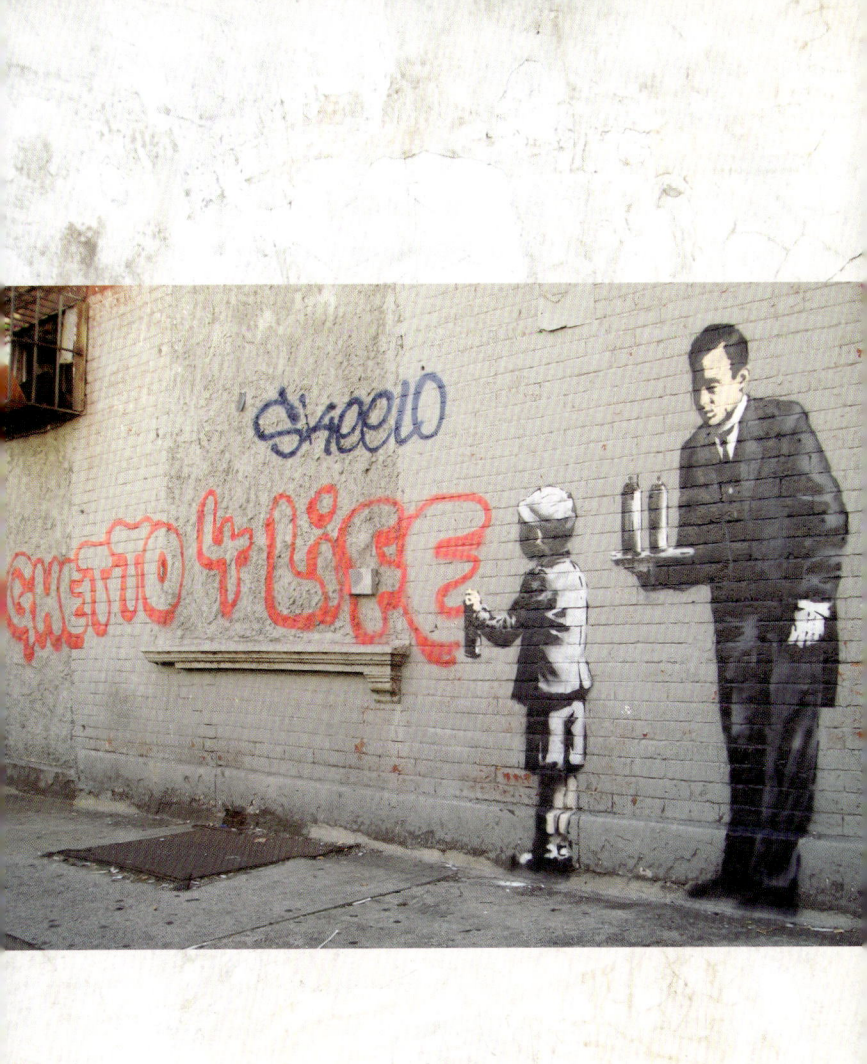

3

WAITING IN VAIN

"There are four basic human needs: food, sleep, sex and revenge."
Banksy.

As ever with Banksy, context is everything. This appeared on a roll-down shutter covering the entrance to Larry Flint's Hustler strip club on 51st Street in Manhattan. The man pictured is waiting for a stripper who presumably worked the night. The leaves falling off the flowers suggest he has waited quite a while and any potential for romance here is wilting, fast. Several dancers from the club came out and posed with the work before the gate was removed 'for safekeeping' that evening.

WHERE IS IT ?
HELL'S KITCHEN,
MANHATTAN,
NYC,
USA.

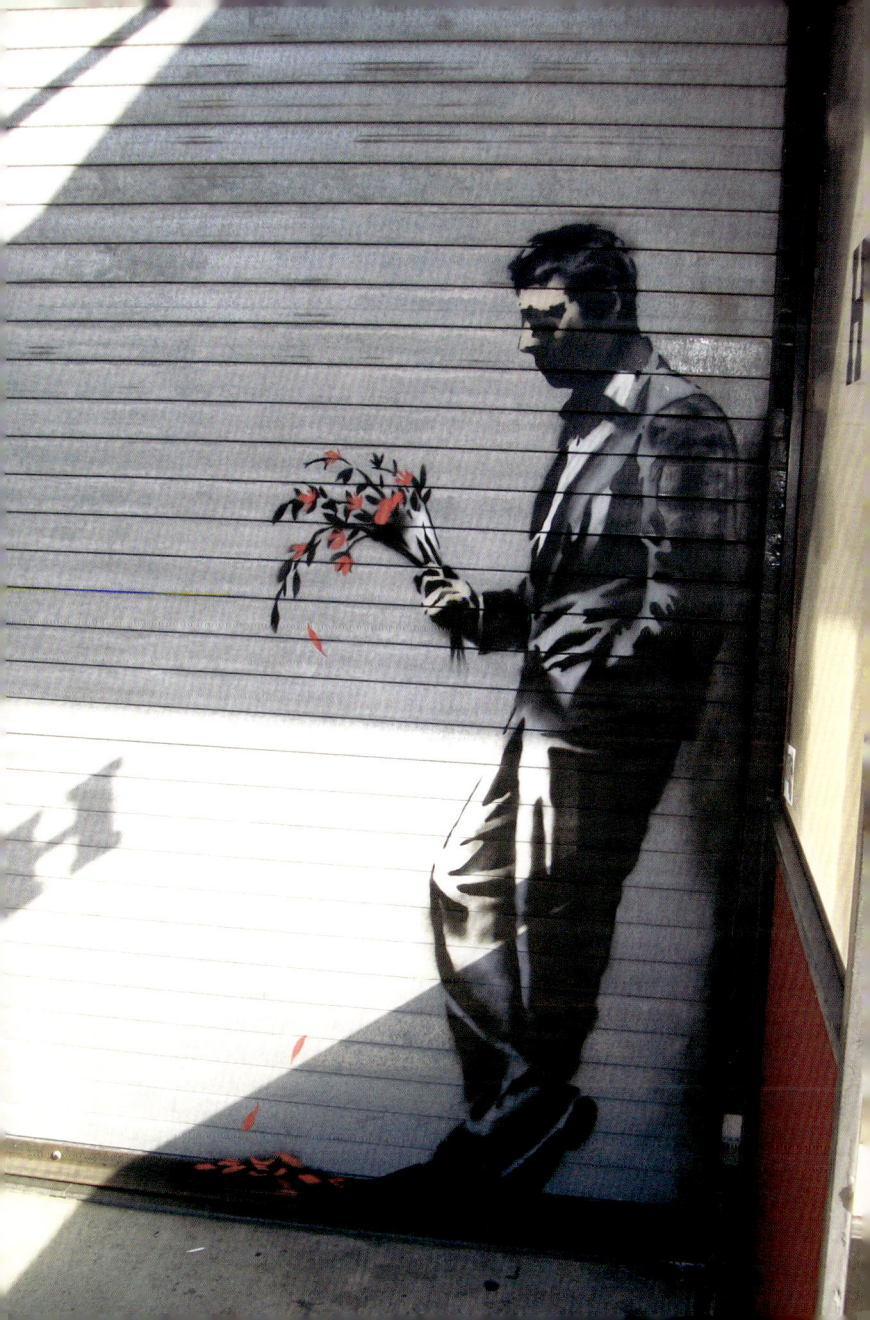

4

JAPANESE SCENE

"One original thought is worth 1,000 meaningless quotes."
Banksy, quoting Diogenes the Cynic.

A wonderful scene of silhouettes of two Japanese ladies conversing, wearing full kimonos with traditional obi sashes. The presence of a parasol and fan, suggest that this is a scene in a relaxing garden. A tagger managed to deface the stencil within an hour of it going up. He was quickly thrown to the ground by a crowd that had assembled. Three Banksy fans, with quick reactions, managed to remove his spraypaint with alcohol wipes.

WHERE IS IT ?
WILLIAMSBURG,
NYC,
USA.
NOW OBSCURED UNDER A
PROTECTIVE ROLLER-SHUTTER.

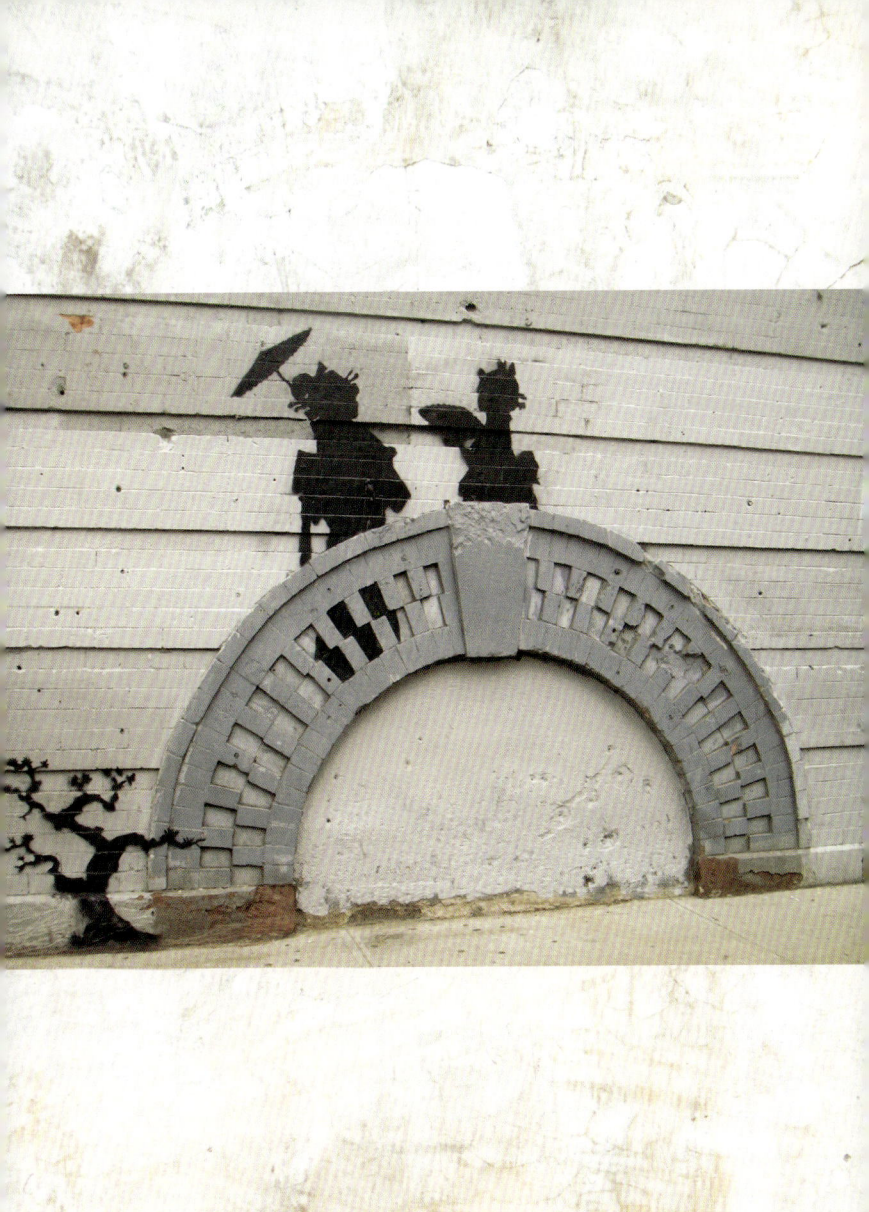

5

SHOE SHINE

"The most sculpted figure in history after Christ."
Banksy.

This ultra-eloquent dig at a major global corporation has it all. Ronald McDonald is having his boots shoe-shined by a man from the lower orders. The look on his face is one of total aristocratic disdain and entitlement. The face was apparently modelled by Banksy after the bust of Hermes by the Ancient Greek sculptor, Praxiteles.

WHERE IS IT ?
BRONX,
NYC,
USA.

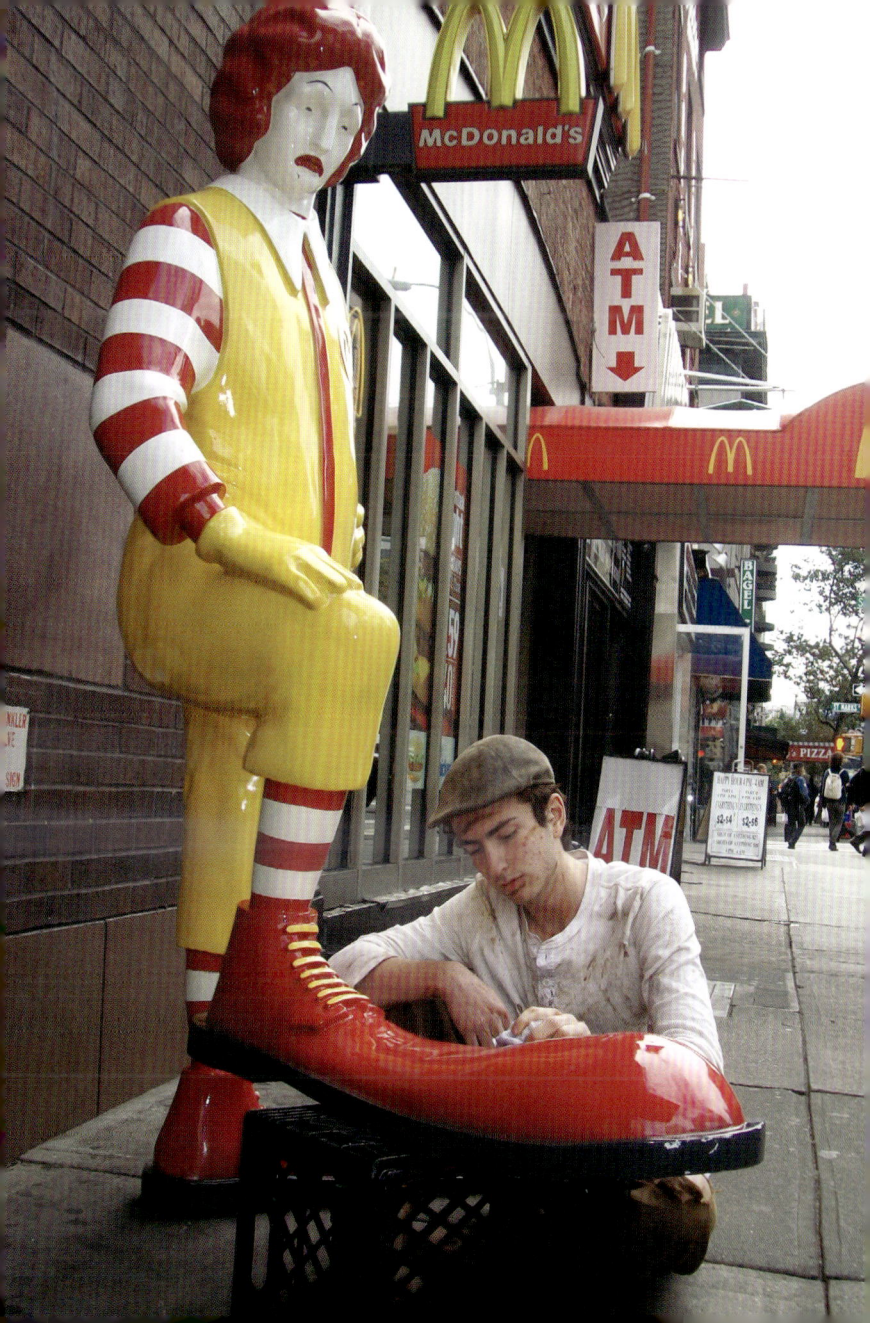

6

SIRENS OF THE LAMBS

"I am having an old friend for dinner."
Dr Hannibal Lecter, *Silence of the Lambs.*

Banksy has made several references in his work to animal cruelty. Here, the cosy comfort of food industry branding and euphemistic language ('Farm Fresh') is in sharp contrast to the violence and horror which will befall these animals very soon. The truck toured the streets of New York, with screams and squeals emanating from inside, for two weeks.

WHERE IS IT ?
MEATPACKING DISTRICT,
MANHATTAN,
NYC,
USA.

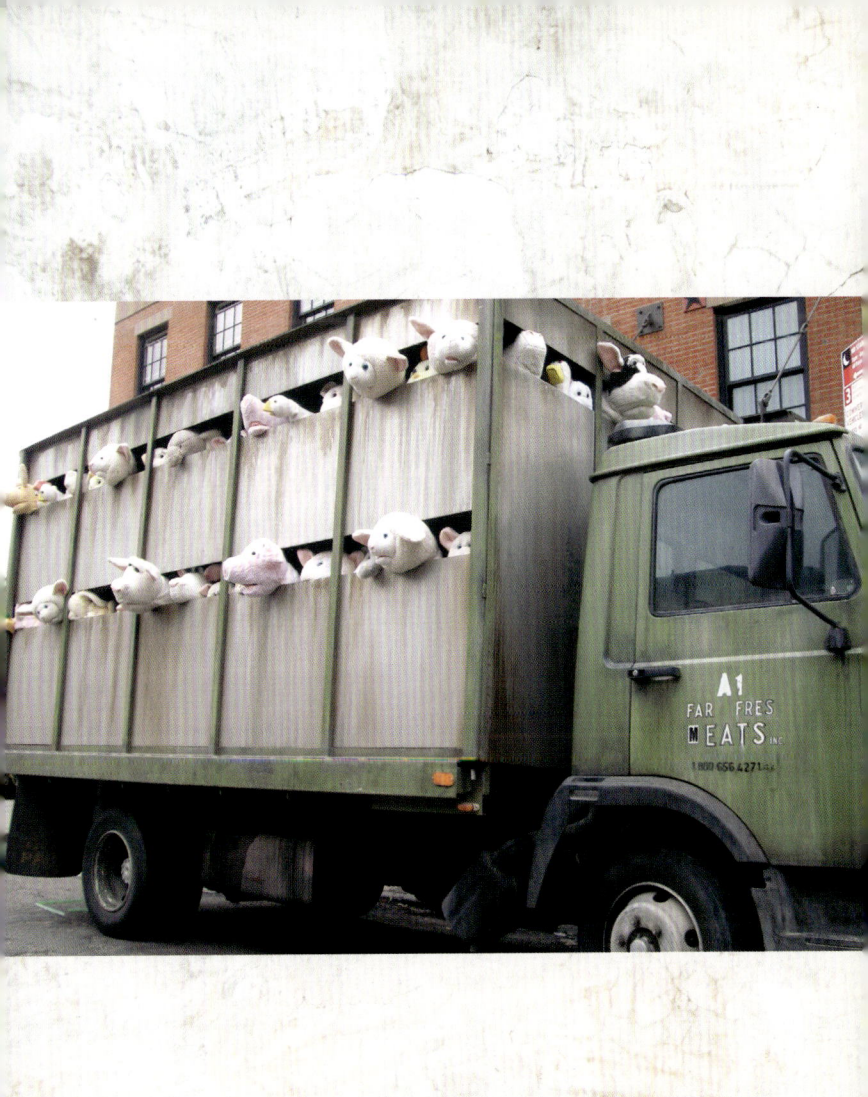

7

ETERNITY

"What we do now echoes in eternity."
Marcus Aurelius, *Meditations*,
written c.170–180 AD.

Banksy wittily takes the Marcus Aurelius quote, written in the neat hand you might be expected to write in for a detention at school, and turns it into a piece on the transience of all things, the most transient of which is street art. It didn't take long for this Banksy to prove its point. By 8pm on the day after its appearance it had already been defaced.

WHERE IS IT ?
WOODSIDE,
QUEENS,
NYC,
USA.
DEFACED SHORTLY AFTER ITS APPEARANCE.

What we do in life echoes in Eternity

8

OS GEMEOS
COLLABORATION

"This is our country. We will occupy it.
These are our streets.
We will occupy them. We are the 99%."
Occupy movement chant.

Brazilian superstar street artists OSGEMEOS (translation: The Twins), collaborated with Banksy on these two mega canvases which appeared on day 18 of the residency in Chelsea, under the Highline. Banksy stated on his website that the 'gallery show' was inspired by the Occupy movement, whose first significant demonstration was Occupy Wall Street, in NYC's Zuccotti Park in 2011.

WHERE IS IT ?
HIGHLINE,
CHELSEA,
NEW YORK,
USA.
THE INSTALLATION WAS REMOVED, WE ASSUME
BY BANKSY OR OSGEMEOS, THE SAME DAY.

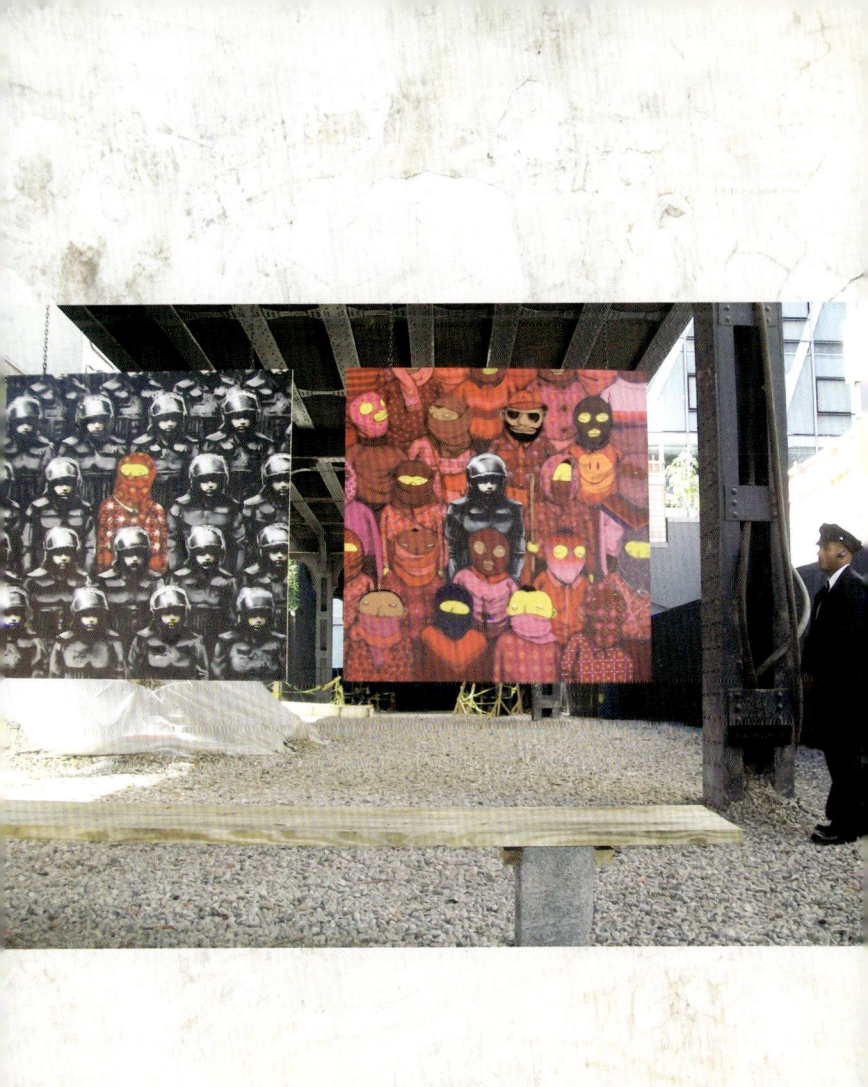

RECENT WORKS

Banksy achieves the unthinkable – a Grade II*
listing – for his Cheltenham surveillance phone box,
an unforgetable image. And then, proving that his
impresario powers are far from diminished, the
astounding Dismaland show, featuring Banksy and
58 other artists. The political themes remain at
the forefront of his work – the plight of the poor
migrants in the Calais Jungle camp inspire the
brilliant Steve Jobs piece and his clever and moving
Cosette piece. Whilst everyone has forgotten
the Palestinians, Banksy shows that he has not,
returning to Gaza for *Kitten* and then, in 2017,
creating the brilliant Walled Off Hotel. In 2018
Banksy created one of his most astonishing pieces
– the remote shredding of one of his works in front
of astonished bidders and journalists at a Sotheby's
auction in London's Mayfair. Then, in 2022, he
reached new heights with his very moving anti-war
works in Ukraine.

GIRL WITH A PIERCED EARDRUM

SPY BOOTH

DISMALAND

SON OF A SYRIAN REFUGEE

KITTEN

COSETTE

BRIDGE FARM PRIMARY SCHOOL

THE WALLED OFF HOTEL

RAGE: THE FLOWER THROWER II

BREAKING NEWS

BREXIT

BASQUIAT

REFUGEE GIRL

CROSSING THE ALPS

LOVE IS IN THE BIN

VENICE IN OIL

DEVOLVED PARLIAMENT

AACHOO!!

CREATE ESCAPE

WE'RE ALL IN THE SAME BOAT

SEAGULL AND CHIPS

HIGH STREET SANDCASTLE

LUXURY RENTALS ONLY

GYMNAST

JUDO

WOMAN IN CURLERS

BANKSY RECENT WORKS

Recently, Banksy's major works have been created in the UK, France, Italy, the West Bank and Ukraine. This period is striking for the absence of works in the USA after the brilliantly effective New York residency.

In England, the triumph of Dismaland took place in the West Country, in Weston-super-Mare. He also created in Bristol and Cheltenham and a great homage to Basquiat was stencilled close to the location of the London Basquiat show. At Sotheby's he created, live, the astonishing *Love is in the Bin*. Banksy then reached new heights with his stunning anti-war works in Ukraine.

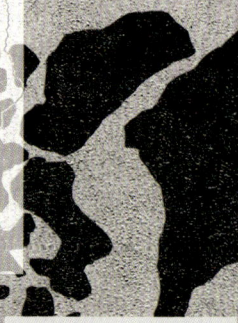

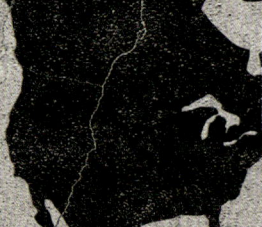

INSTALLATION

WESTERN-SUPER-MARE
❸ Dismaland,
Tropicana Lido, Weston-Super-Mare, UK.
21st August-27th September 2015.

READING
⓳ *Create Escape*,
Reading.

CHELTENHAM
❷ *Spy Booth*,
Suburb of Cheltenham.

BRISTOL
❶ *Girl With Pierced Eardrum*,
Albion Docks.

❼ *Bridge Farm Primary School*,
Whitchurch.

⓲ *AACHOO!!*,
Totterdown.

LONDON
❻ *Cosette*,
Knightsbridge.

⓬ *Basquiat*,
Barbican.

⓯ *Love is in the Bin*,
Sotheby's, Mayfair.

⓱ *Devolved Parliament*,
Sotheby's, Mayfair.

EAST ANGLIA
❷⓿ We're All in the Same Boat.
❷❶ Seagull and Chips,
❷❷ High Street Sandcastle,
All Lowestoft.

❷❸ Luxury Rentals Only,
Cromer.

CALAIS
❹ Son of a Syrian Refugee,
Jungle Camp.

UKRAINE
❷❹ ❷❺ ❷❻
Banksy's works in Kyiv, Borodyanka and Hostomel.

VENICE
❶❻ Venice in Oil,
St Mark's Square.

BETHLEHEM
❽ Walled-Off Hotel,
West Bank.

❾ Rage: The Flower Thrower,
West Bank.

❿ Breaking News,
West Bank.

GAZA STRIP
❺ Kitten,
Bet Hanoun.

PARIS
❶❸ Refugee Girl,
18th Arrondissement.

❶❹ Crossing the Alps,
19th Arrondissement.

DOVER
❶❶ Brexit,
Ferry Port Approaches.

1

GIRL WITH A PIERCED EARDRUM

"The artist has also made a tongue-in-cheek reference to the burger van opposite, with the caption 'Gallery cafe open Monday to Sunday 8am to 2pm'."

Bristol Post.

Back on his home turf, a brilliant parody of Vermeer's wonderful *Girl with a Pearl Earring*, using a yellow ADT security alarm box in place of the pearl, and retitled, appositely, *Girl With a Pierced Eardrum*. Another Banksy side-swipe at the paranoia associated with the security industry.

WHERE IS IT ?
ALBION DOCKS,
BRISTOL,
UK.
STILL THERE.

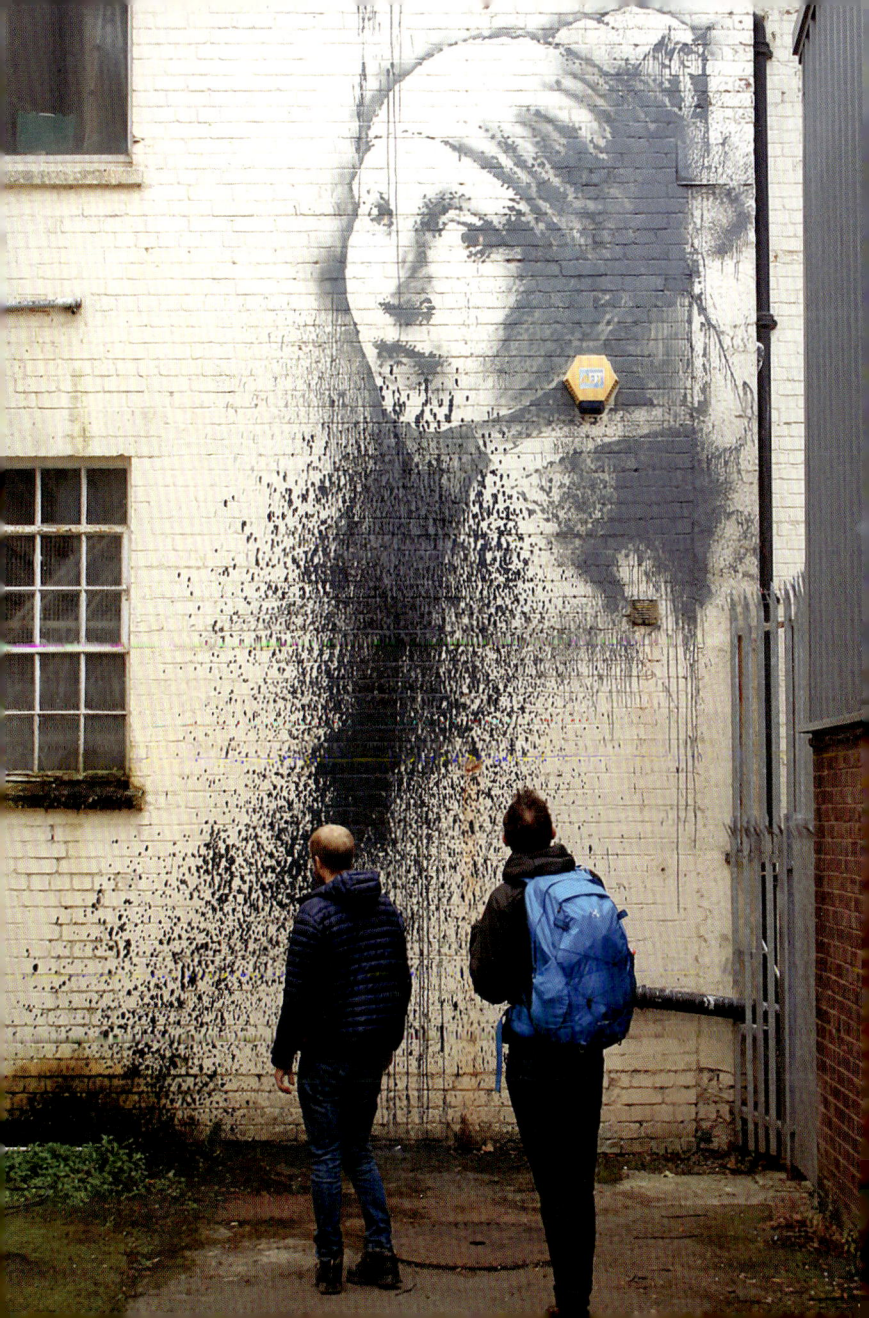

❷

SPY BOOTH

"Surprised...when I did art at school I got an 'ungraded'."
Banksy, in response to the news that this artwork would be listed Grade II*.

It may seem strange that this surveillance piece should appear by a phone box, painted onto the side of a very ordinary house in Cheltenham, a rather sleepy, conservative, quintessentially English market town in Gloucestershire. Not so strange when you realise that GCHQ (Government Communications Headquarters) is just three miles away. GCHQ is the UK government's ears and eyes across the globe.

WHERE IS IT ?
CHELTENHAM,
UK.
LISTED GRADE II*, MEANING ANY TAGGING,
OR BUFFING, IS A CRIMINAL OFFENCE.
MYSTERIOUSLY REMOVED IN 2016.

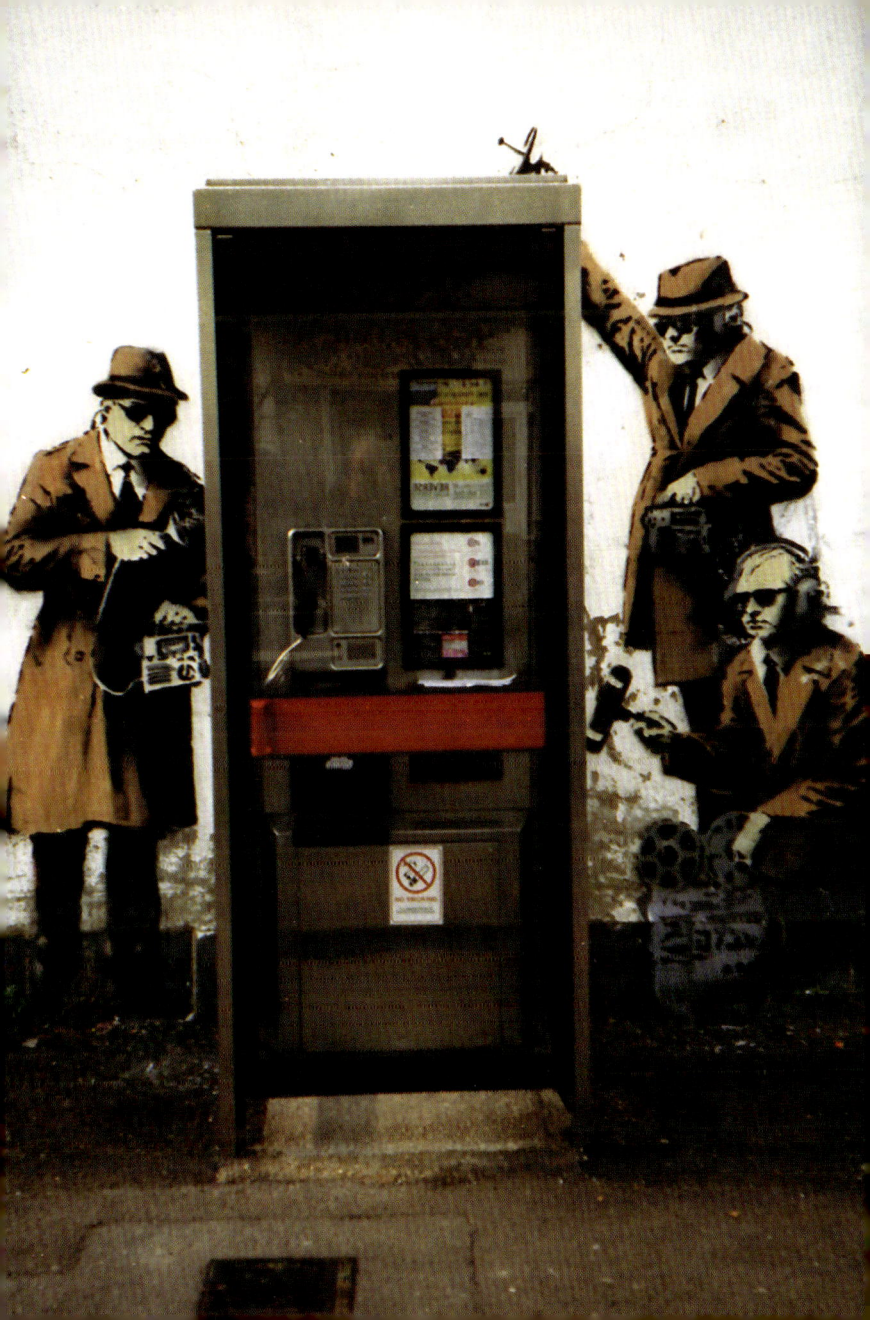

3

DISMALAND

"The following are strictly prohibited in the Park – spray paint, marker pens, knives and legal representatives of the Walt Disney Corporation."
Dismaland brochure.

Banksy has form as an impressario-provocateur. Dismaland, however, surpassed all previous efforts. Billed as a 'Bemusement Park' and as 'The UK's most disappointing new visitor attraction', the name was a polemical dig at Disney. Inside, the works of 58 artists and activists were on show, including Damien Hirst, Jimmy Cauty, Bäst, Espo and Jenny Holzer. Dismaland received 150,000 visitors and contributed over £20 million to the local economy.

WHERE IS IT ?
TROPICANA LIDO, SEAFRONT,
WESTON-SUPER-MARE,
UK.
RIGHT: SHOWER SCREEN BY BANKSY.
OVERLEAF: AERIAL VIEW OF THE PARK.

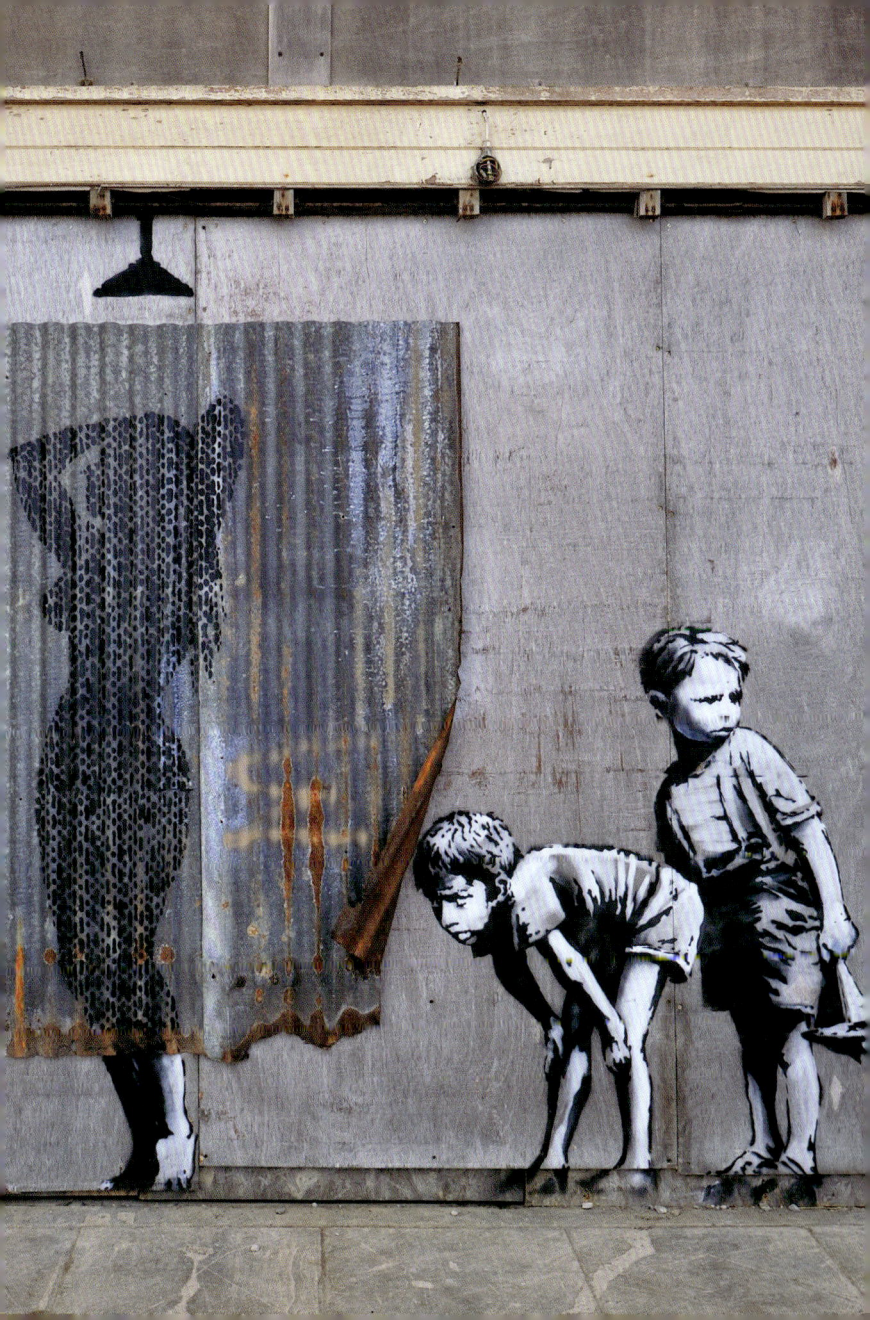

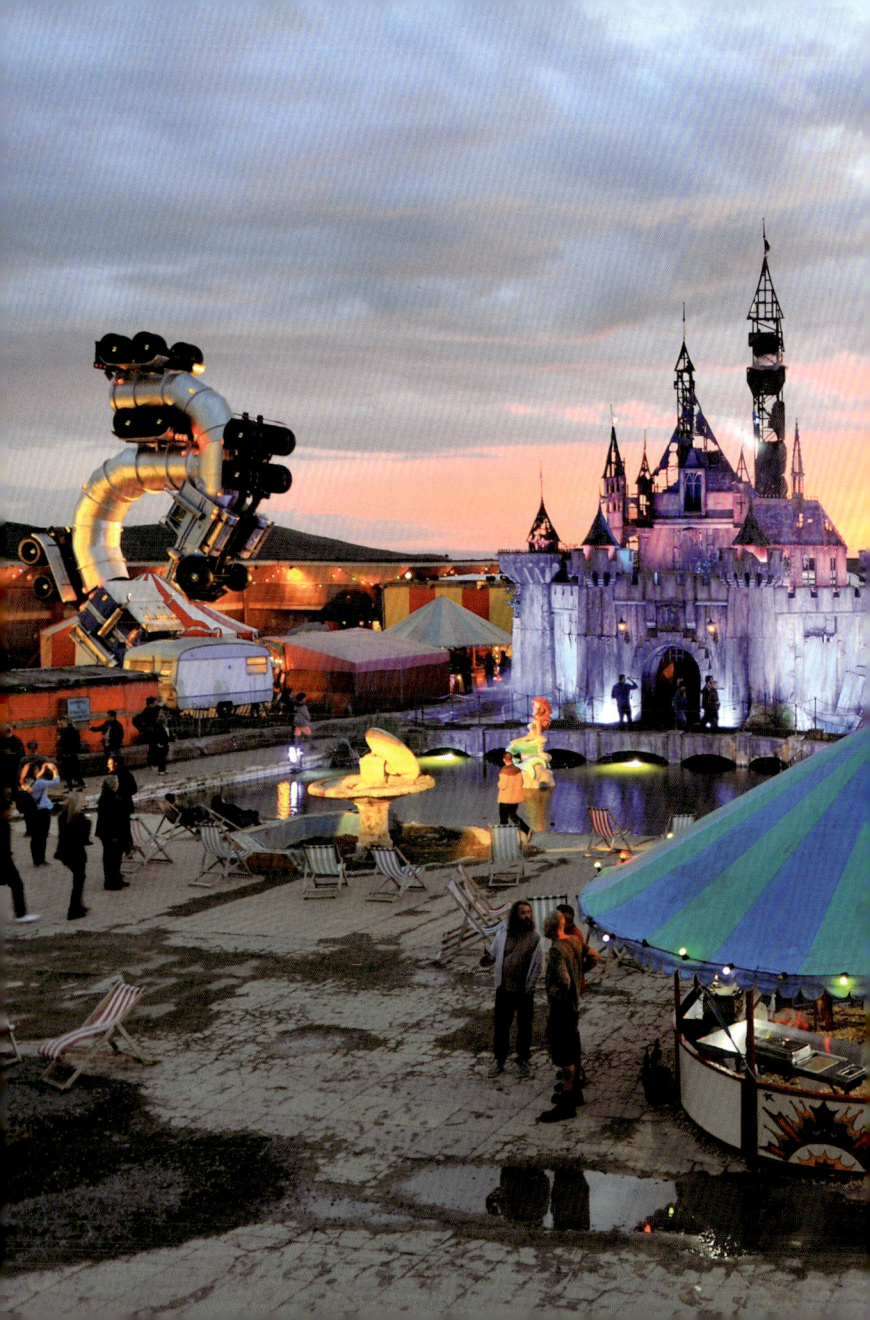

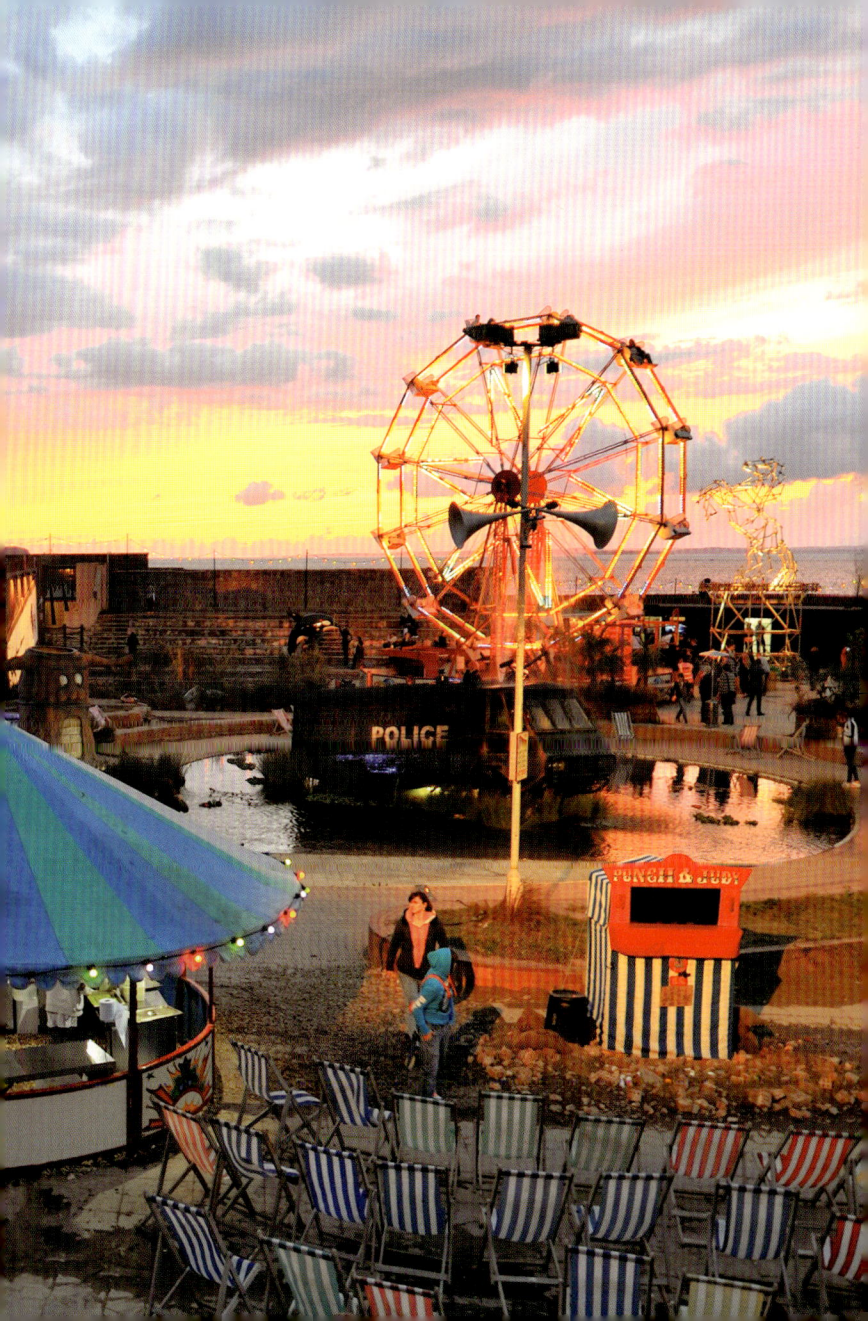

4

SON OF A SYRIAN REFUGEE

"Being the richest man in the cemetery doesn't matter to me. Going to bed at night saying we've done something wonderful, that's what matters."

Steve Jobs.

Steve Jobs, the legendary co-founder of the world's most successful computer company (and, in 2015 when this piece was created also the world's most valuable company), was the son of a Muslim Syrian refugee to the USA. The piece challenged the viewer: "Look at me. I may be a migrant, but I am also an individual with brilliant ideas who will transform your world for the better."

WHERE IS IT ?
'JUNGLE' CAMP,
LANDFILL SITE,
CALAIS,
FRANCE.

118

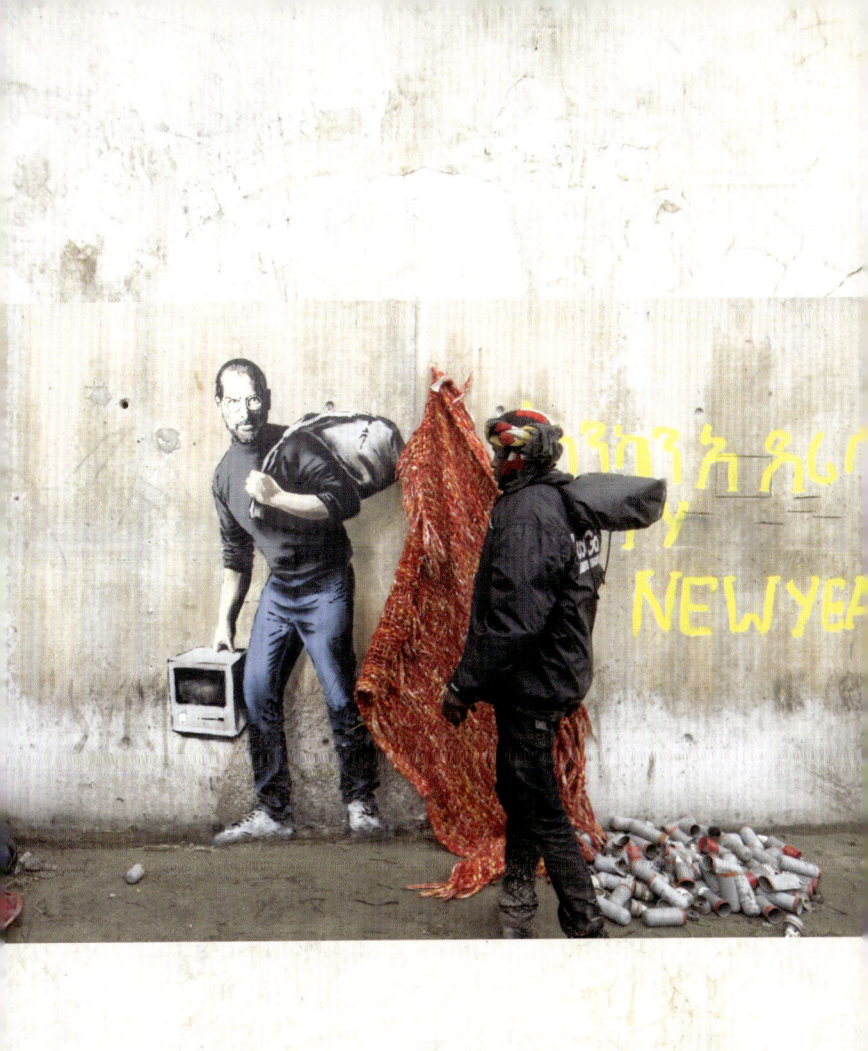

5

KITTEN

"I wanted to highlight the destruction in Gaza by posting photos on my website – but on the Internet people only look at pictures of kittens."
Banksy's website, 2015.

In 2014 the Israeli Armed Forces launched an operation, ostensibly in response to Hamas rocket attacks, called Operation Protective Edge. The result was 2,104 people killed in Gaza, with 69% of deaths, according to the UN, being civilians. On the Israeli side 67 soldiers and 6 civilians were killed. The side of a house on which Banksy created this image was one of 18,000 destroyed in the attacks.

WHERE IS IT ?
BEIT HANOUN TOWN,
NORTHERN GAZA STRIP.

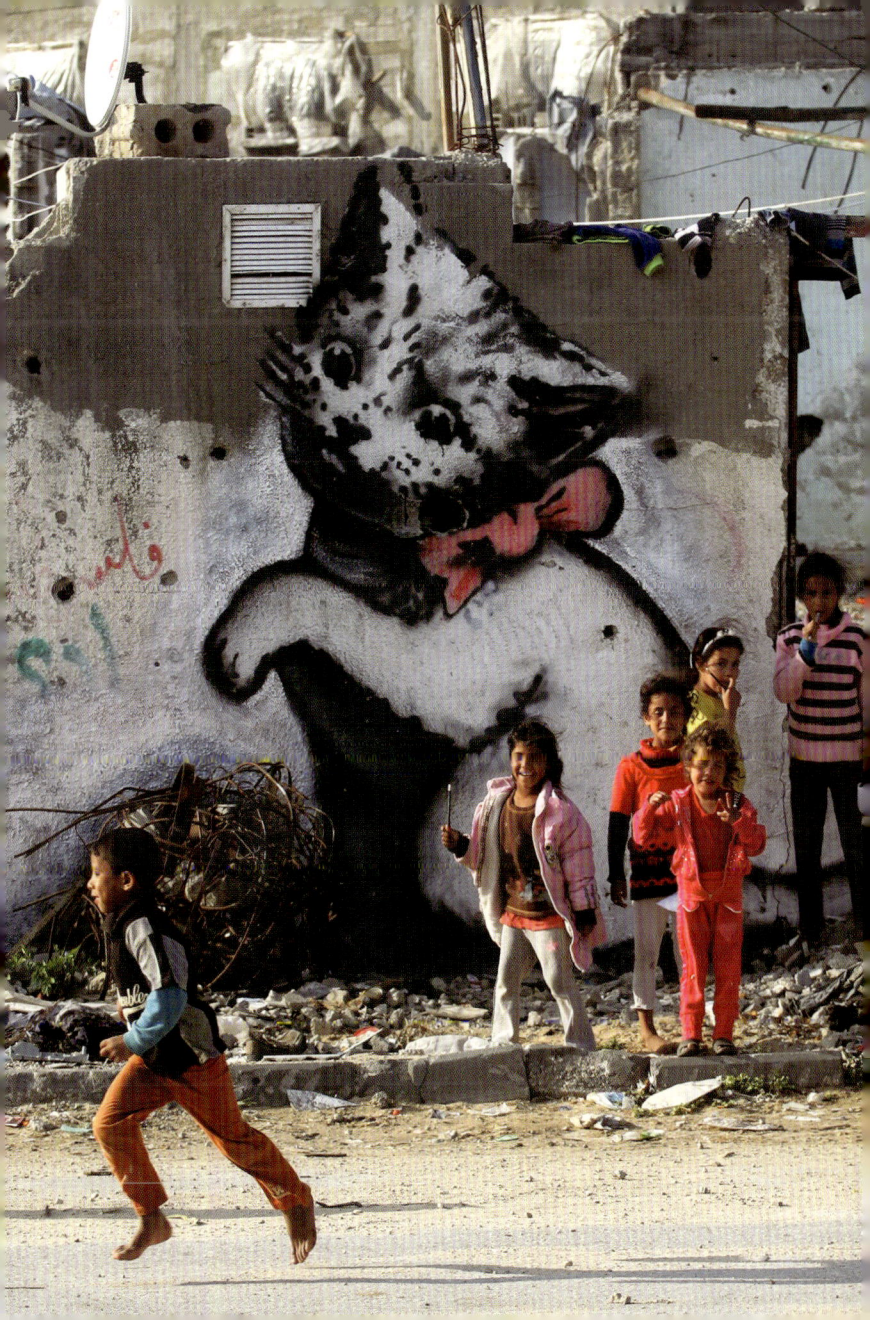

6

COSETTE

"At the end of the day, you're another day older, and that's all you can say, about the life of the poor."
Les Misérables, the Musical.

Banksy's piece appeared on a scaffold hoarding opposite the French Embassy in London in January 2016. The QR code to the left of the image directed viewers to a graphic video of French police raids on the Calais migrant 'Jungle' on 5th January 2016, when tear gas, rubber bullets and concussion grenades were used. The image of Cosette is, of course, from the world-beating musical based on Victor Hugo's novel, *Les Misérables*.

WHERE IS IT ?
KNIGHTSBRIDGE,
LONDON,
UK.
BOARDED UP WITHIN 24 HOURS AND REMOVED
BY CHEVAL ESTATES, THE LUXURY PROPERTY
DEVELOPERS WHO HIRED THE SCAFFOLD.

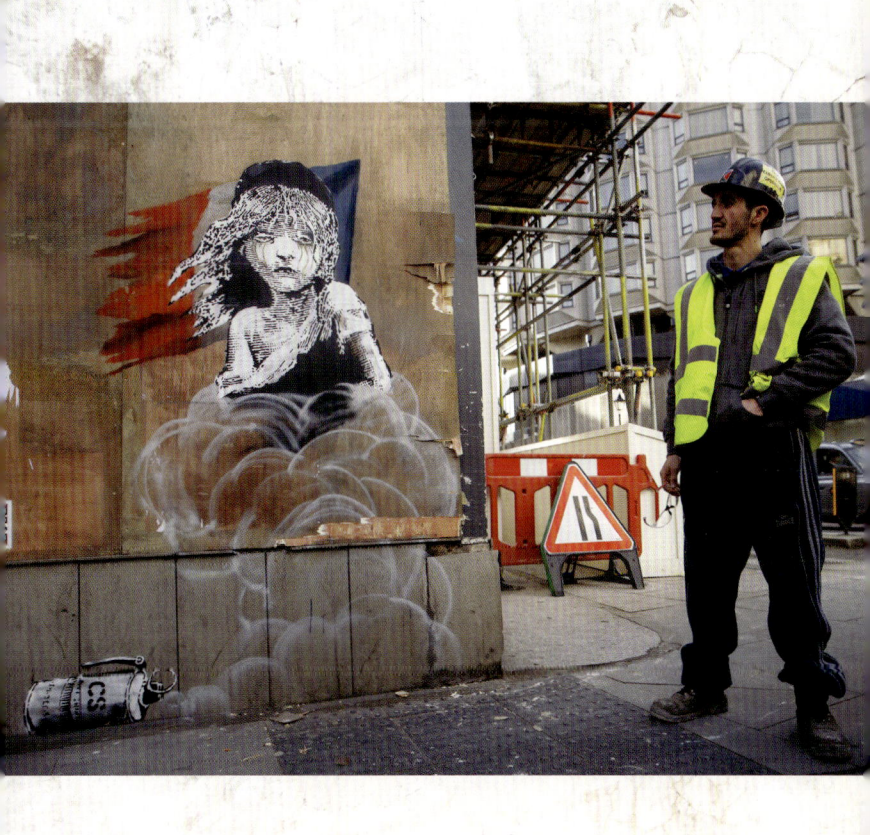

❼

BRIDGE FARM PRIMARY SCHOOL

"Remember it's always easier to get forgiveness than permission".
Banksy's note to the children of Bridge Farm Primary School, Bristol.

In 2016, the pupils from Bridge Farm Primary decided to rename their school houses after five renowned Bristolians, one of whom was Banksy. They sent Banksy a letter telling him of their plans and went away for their half-term holidays. To their delight, on their return they found this very funny mural by way of thanks from the artist, together with a note with the words of wisdom above.

WHERE IS IT ?
BRIDGE FARM PRIMARY SCHOOL,
BRISTOL,
UK.
STILL THERE!

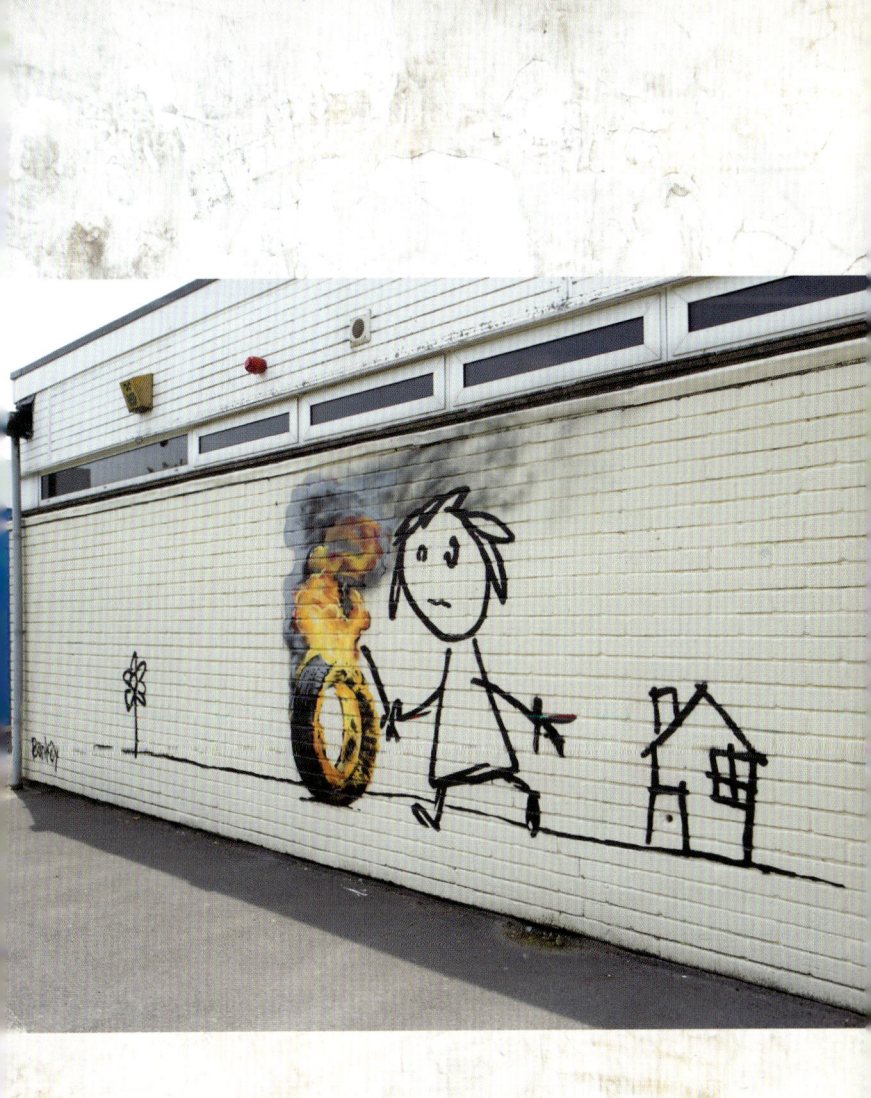

8

THE WALLED OFF HOTEL

"The hotel with the worst view in the world."
Banksy, 2017.

Banksy returned to the West Bank dividing wall for his brilliant installation of 2017 – a hotel full of his art, where guests can stay. A brilliantly witty play on New York's top-flight Waldorf Hotel, the installation is a cutting reminder of how the West enjoys its luxury, whilst forgetting the plight of the desperate, encarcerated Palestinians. Following pages show artworks from the interior.

WHERE IS IT ?
OVERLOOKING THE
ISRAELI 'SECURITY BARRIER',
BETHLEHEM,
WEST BANK.
YOU CAN BOOK TO STAY!

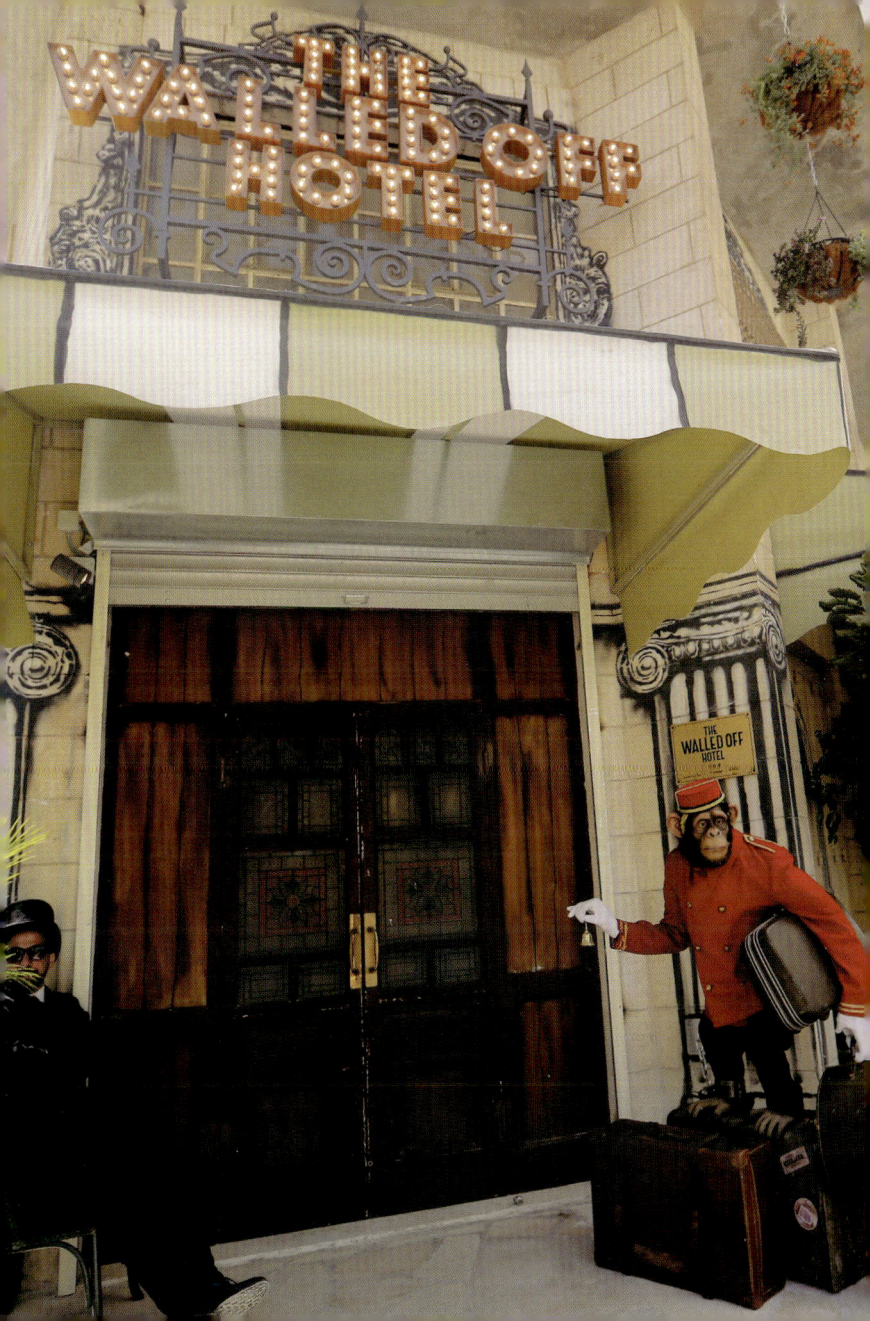

9

RAGE: THE FLOWER THROWER II

"If you are not completely baffled, then you don't understand."
West Bank history video, The Walled Off Hotel Museum, 2017.

A wonderful replay of one of Banksy's iconic first works in the West Bank, showing a rioting youth throwing a bouquet of flowers in lieu of a rock. The use of a real vase with real flowers is classic, witty Banksy. The image is one of the most powerful, visceral calls to peace ever created.

WHERE IS IT ?
THE WALLED OFF HOTEL LOBBY,
BETHLEHEM,
WEST BANK.

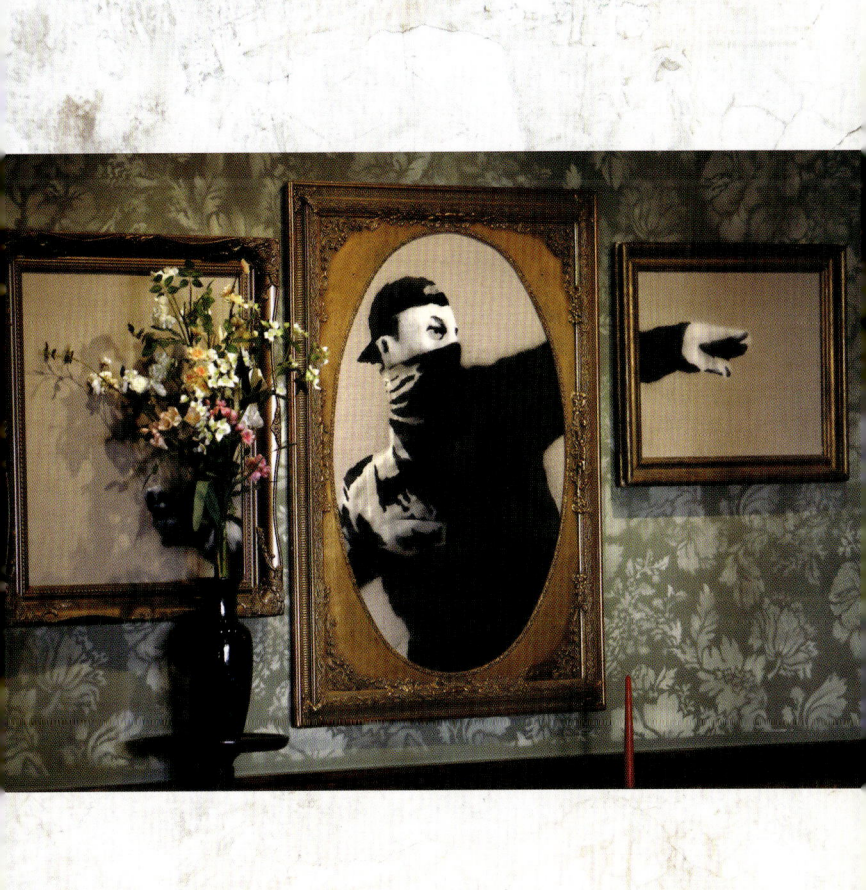

⑩

BREAKING NEWS

"Walls are hot right now, but I was into them long before Trump made it cool."
Banksy, 2017.

A fake flat-screen TV, with an image of a Palestinian woman about to express her desperation by throwing rocks, rather challengingly here, at the hotel guest. Banksy forces the thought that Palestinians are living through hell, not least by showing 'breaking news' as actually breaking the glass of the TV screen. Wake up, he seems to be saying, this isn't news as entertainment, this is happening right here, right now.

WHERE IS IT ?
THE WALLED OFF HOTEL GUEST ROOM AT THE
WALLED OFF HOTEL,
BETHLEHEM,
WEST BANK.

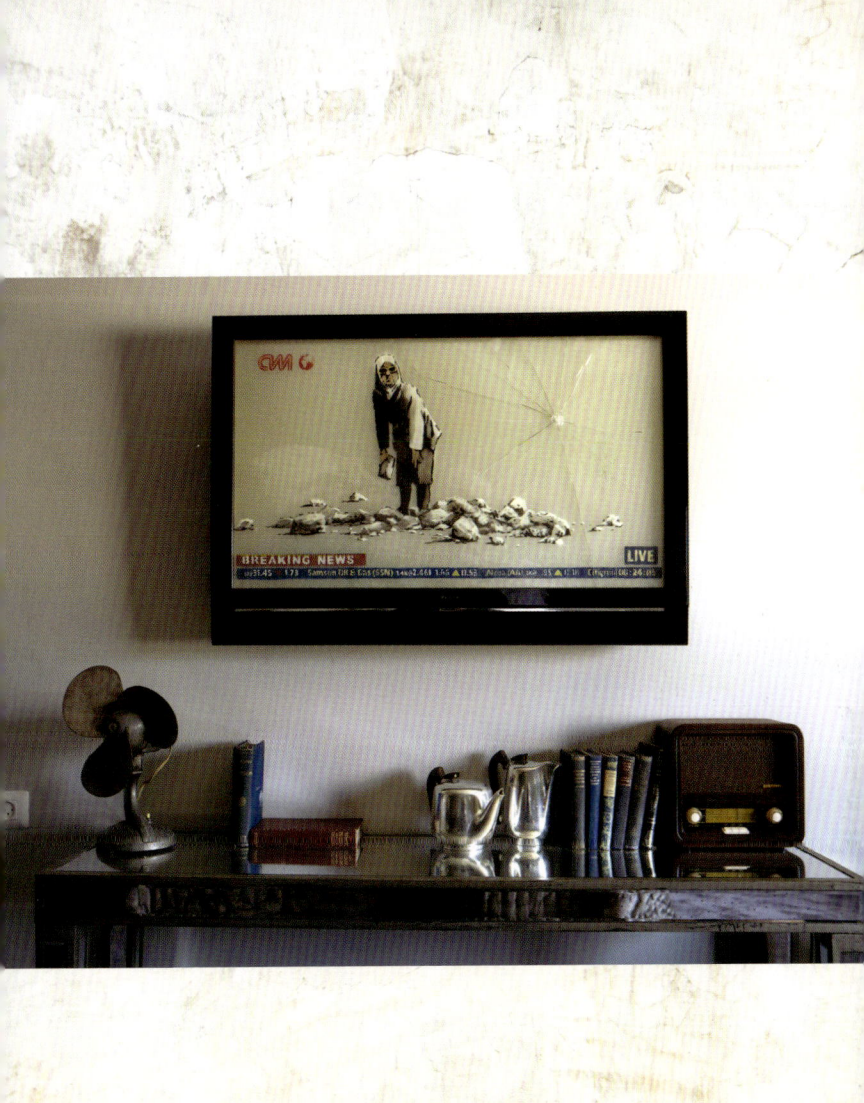

⑪

BREXIT

"The stars stand for the ideals of unity, solidarity and harmony among the peoples of Europe." EU's website.

On June 23rd, 2016, the UK voted in a referendum to leave the EU. A year later, on 29th March, 2017, Article 50, beginning the formal process of leaving, was triggered by the UK government. This was during the fraught run up to the French presidential elections, which saw the right-wing anti-EU candidate, Marie Le Pen, gaining in the polls. On the morning of the French election, Sunday May 7th, this Banksy appeared in Dover, Britain's gateway to Europe. As usual, Banksy has proved himself a master of paradox. The mural appeared on a building next to the ferry port which was slated for demolition. It was cars and lorries going *to* and trading *with* Europe that would be best placed to see it. And this willful act of self-destruction is being carefully undertaken by a conscientious worker – it was the working class vote, particularly in towns like Dover, which led to the winning Brexit vote. Banksy at his clever, subtle best.

WHERE IS IT ?
YORK STREET,
DOVER FERRY PORT APPROACHES.
MYSTERIOUSLY WHITEWASHED IN AUGUST, 2019.

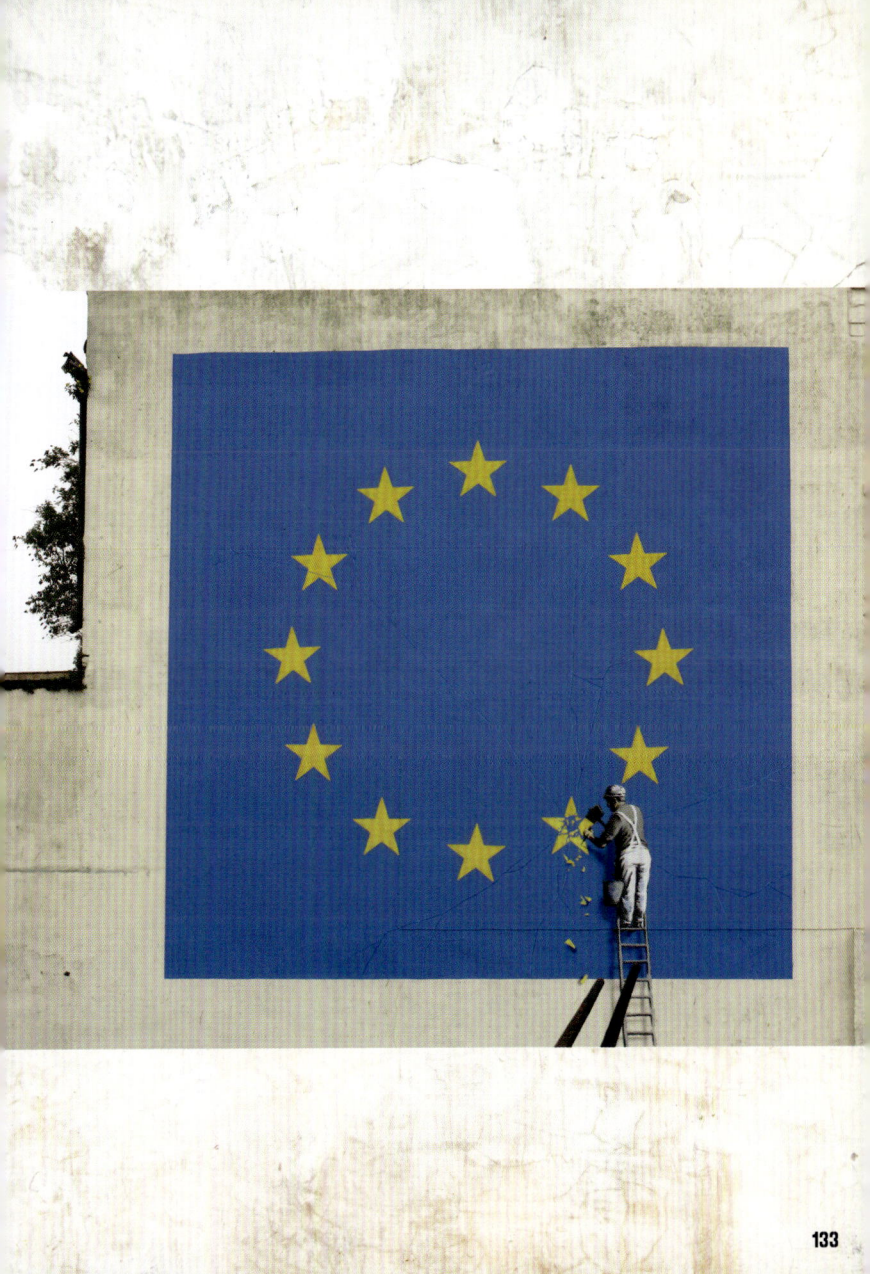

12

BASQUIAT

"Major new Basquiat show opens at the Barbican – a place that is normally very keen to clean any graffiti from its walls."
Banksy's Instagram.

Banksy loves nothing more than mocking the British middle classes for their hypocrisy. This piece appeared before the opening of the first major show of Basquiat's work in the UK, in the City's major art centre, bang in the middle of the financial district. The people now fawning over the New York graffiti artist's work, would have been those who would have applauded the police stopping and searching a black man walking near the gallery just because he looked, in their eyes, 'suspicious'. Young black guys in London are eleven times more likely to be searched by the Metropolitan Police than whites, according to the UK's official Equality and Human Rights Commission. Basquiat would have been one of those guys. The piece, inspired by Basquiat's 1982 *Boy and Dog in a Johnnypump*, is clearly an homage from one brilliant artist to another.

WHERE IS IT ?
BARBICAN,
THE CITY (FINANCIAL DISTRICT)
LONDON.

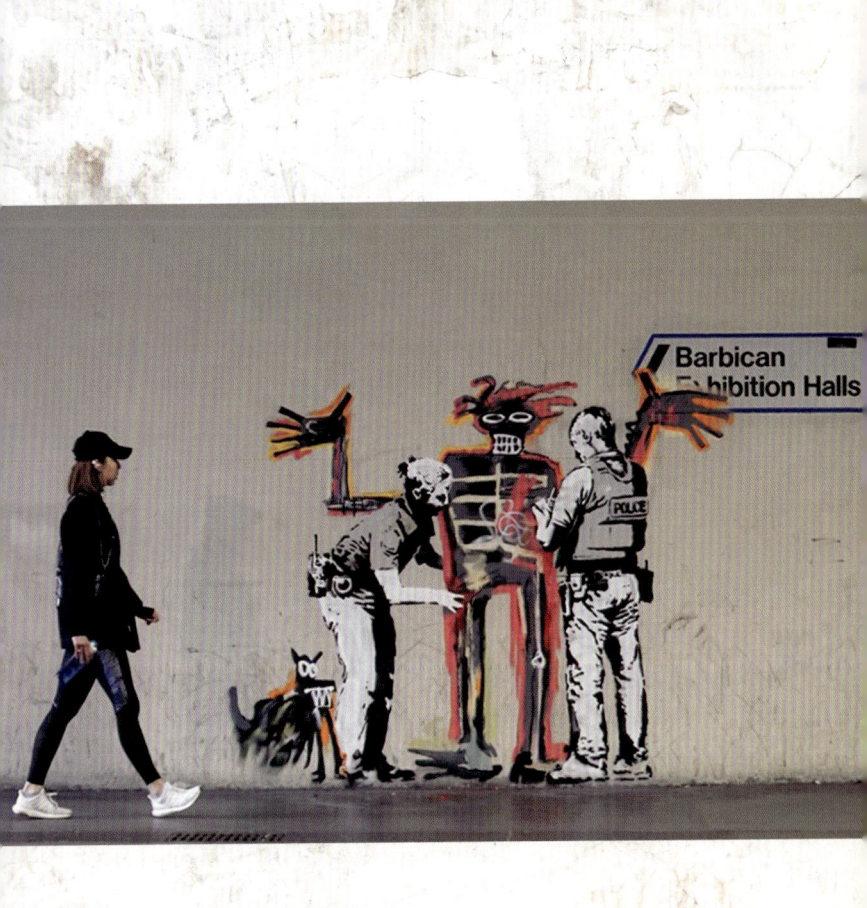

⓭

REFUGEE GIRL

"June 20th is the day the world commemorates the strength, courage and perseverance of millions of refugees."
UNHCR

At the end of June, 2018, Banksy blitzed Paris with a series of works around the city celebrating 50 years since the 1968 Paris uprisings, declaring the city the birthplace of modern stencil art, but also highlighting the plight of refugees as new right-wing measures under Macron were introduced. This piece appeared on World Refugee Day outside a closed centre for migrants. The residents were simply thrown out on the street. Banksy's ability to capture the poignancy of childhood is very much in evidence here. The little girl is trying to make a home in an increasingly fascistic environment, but her improvised pink wallpaper is not enough to cover the threatening swastika. She doesn't have the cheeky look of some of Banksy's other child artists; her look is rather one of fear at very possibly being deported if caught. Her teddy, it would seem, is her only comfort. Banksy is asking: how can we treat child refugees so inhumanly?

WHERE IS IT ?
PORTE DE LA CHAPELLE,
18TH ARRONDISSEMENT,
PARIS.

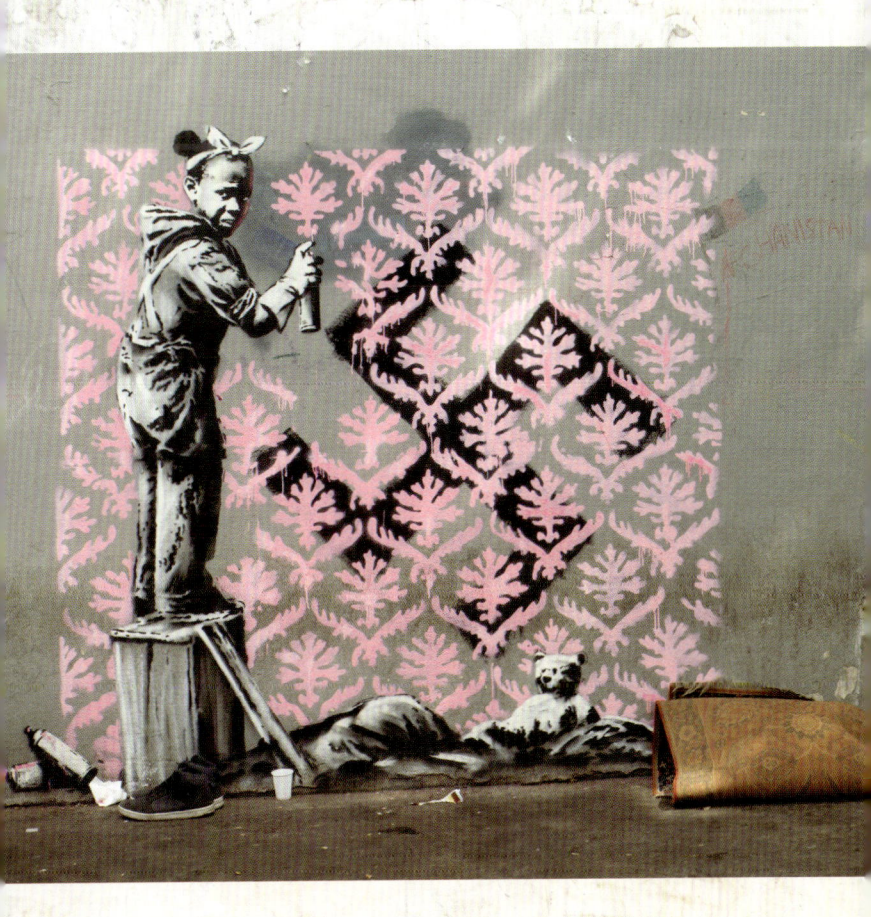

⑭

CROSSING THE ALPS

"*Liberté, Égalité, Cable TV.*"
Banksy's Instagram account

Jacques-Louis David's 1801 painting *Napoleon Crossing the Alps*, is referenced here, Banksy at his visually eloquent best. The stunning picture of France's most iconic leader was also Bonaparte's favourite; he had five copies made. In David's painting, Napoleon is heroically pointing the way towards the invasion of Italy. In Banksy's piece, Napoleon is wrapped in a red arabic headscarf, and the heroic gesture is absent. The piece seems to be a comment on how, with the absurd bans on the niqab and burkini, France has abandoned its true spirit, is in effect blind to what it is doing. The horse, far from charging forwards, looks as though it will unseat its rider. Banksy loves his historical allusions: he will have known that Napoleon was a great emancipator of oppressed minorities, notably of Jews, and that his 1804 penal code decriminalised gay and lesbian sex. Banksy seems to be asking France: where oh where are your liberal Napoleonic and 1968 instincts? The choice of the image also references the fact that many refugees arrive in France via the alpine passes.

WHERE IS IT ?
AVENUE FLANDRE,
19TH ARRONDISSEMENT,
PARIS.

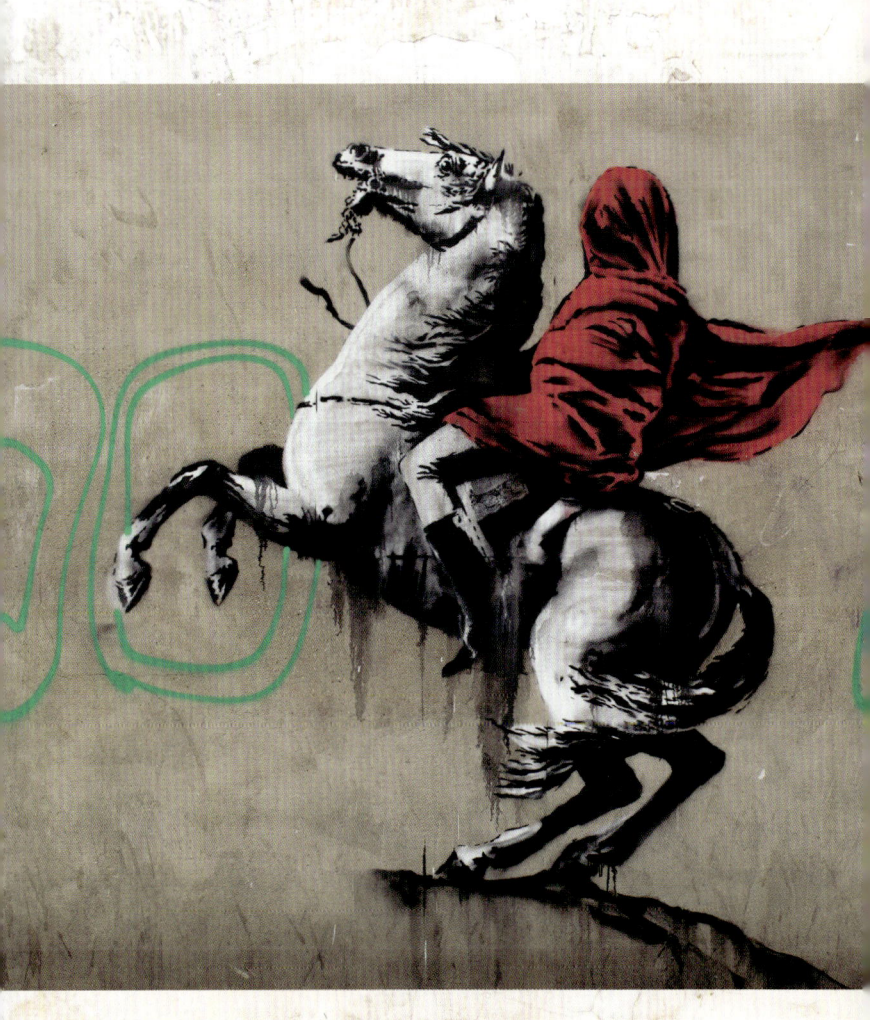

⑮

LOVE IS IN THE BIN

"...in the process of 'destroying' the artwork, a new one was created."
Sothebys.com

The date: 5th October, 2018; the location: Sotheby's auction house in London. The lot was an authenticated Banksy, *Girl with Red Balloon*. Then, as the hammer went down with the top bid of £1.03 million (inc. commission), the picture started shredding before the astonished crowd. Banksy had not just pranked Sotheby's, but the entire art world and its bizarre sense of what constitutes art and value. A shredder, hidden in the frame, had been set off remotely. But things didn't go according to plan. The shredder jammed, with only half the picture destroyed, leaving the lonely heart balloon still in frame. The astonishing stunt made headlines around the world: the first artwork in history to have been created, live, during an auction. Banksy renamed the work *Love is in the Bin*. The buyer, far from being distraught at the wrecking of her purchase, was thrilled. Estimates suggested it was now worth twice what she had just paid (it in fact sold for £18.5 million at Sotheby's in 2021). Banksy has the last laugh: the world of 'high' art clearly values rubbish more than the art itself.

WHERE?
SOTHEBY'S AUCTION HOUSE, MAYFAIR,
LONDON.

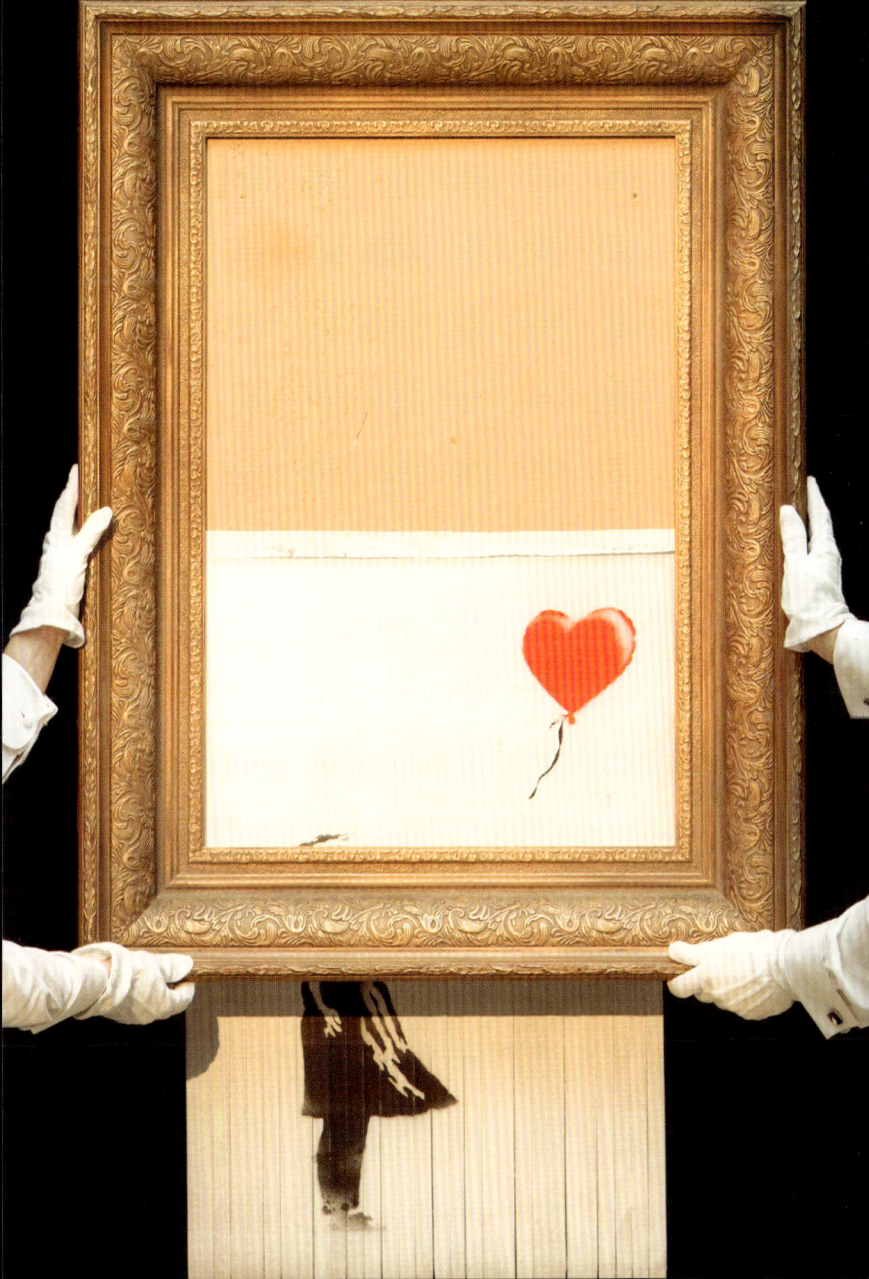

⑯
VENICE IN OIL

"Despite being the largest and most prestigious art event in the world, for some reason I've never been invited." **Banksy's Instagram, on the Biennale.**

On the 22nd May 2019, during the Biennale, Banksy trundled a street vendor's art trolley into St. Mark's Square, opening it up to reveal this series of canvases. Classic scenes from Canaletto of the Rialto, Grand Canal and San Giorgio Maggiore are swamped by a vast cruise ship. It's a brilliant critique of the Venetian authorities trashing their own – the world's most beautiful – city. Banksy also makes an environmental point: these cruise liners not only have a huge carbon footprint, they leech oil into the lagoon's sensitive ecosystems. *Venice in Oil* isn't just a deliciously sardonic pun, with its art scholarship overtones; it's also framed in black, in the manner of invitations to funerals. Banksy (for we think it was he), was bundled off by the police as his display was unauthorized. They didn't bother to look twice at the work. It was all filmed for his Instagram. Effortlessly, Banksy once again cocks a snook at ridiculous authority figures, strutting about in their silly uniforms.

WHERE?
ST. MARK'S SQUARE,
VENICE.

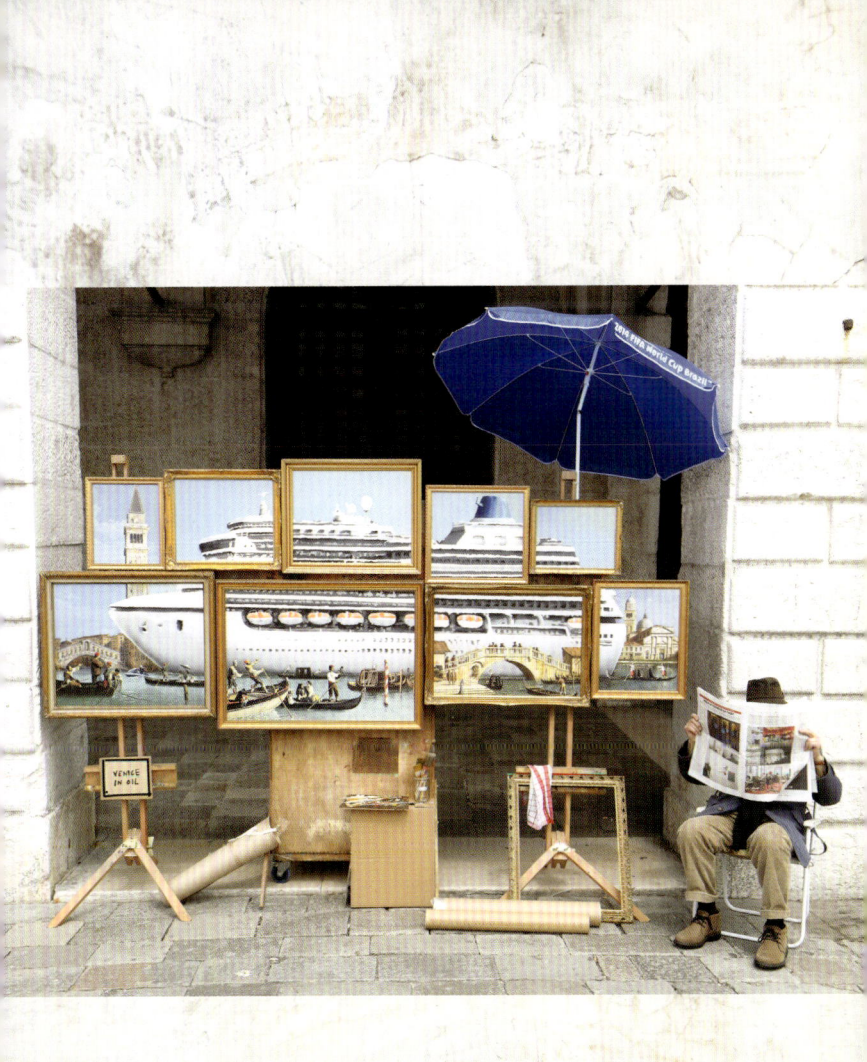

17

DEVOLVED PARLIAMENT

"Record price for a Banksy painting [£9.9 million] set at auction tonight. Shame I didn't still own it." Banksy's Instagram.

When Banksy first revealed this huge oil – in 2009 – it seemed a witty comment on the uselessness of the UK Parliament. After all, only one of the 650 chimps/MPs, had warned against the crash of 2007/08. But if they seemed simian then, how about in 2019, when they had spent three years trying to rip Britain out of the EU, yet could not agree how to do it? One can't imagine a better depiction of their mind-numbing inability to lead the nation. If anything, compared to many MPs in the House of Commons, the chimps appear rather distinguished. The owner, realising it had resonance, lent it back to the Bristol Museum to mark the planned exit of Britain from the EU on 29th March 2019. But the chimps again didn't manage to agree and extended the deadline: the absurdity of it all made it time to sell. The Banksy was now *the* image which defined this moment in Britain's history. Sotheby's, the auctioneers, were bullish, and suggested an estimate of £1.5m – £2m. On the day, bidding took just 13 minutes, with the hammer going down at £9,879,500.00.

WHERE?
TWO PORTERS HANGING *DEVOLVED PARLIAMENT* IN SOTHEBY'S AUCTION HOUSE, IN PREPARATION FOR VIEWING PRIOR TO ITS RECORD-BREAKING SALE ON OCTOBER 3RD, 2019.

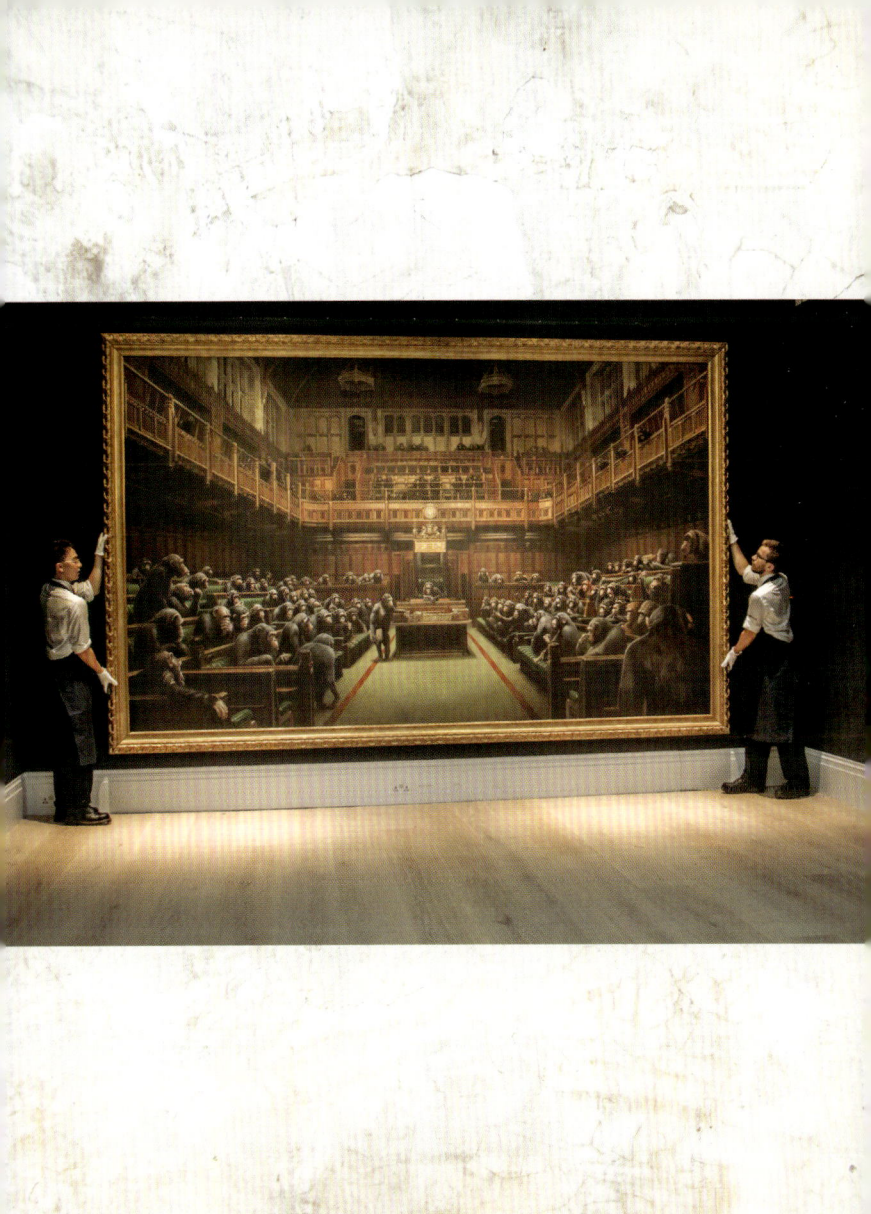

⑱

AACHOO!!

"Banksy's "Aachoo!!" post has already been liked over 2 million times on Instagram." CNN, on 11th December 2020.

If ever a situation called for the Banksy treatment, it was surely the Covid-19 pandemic that spread around the world in 2019-2021. We had to wait until 10th December 2020 for this brilliant piece, which appeared on the side of a house in Bristol. As ever with Banksy there are layers of possible interpretations. Is the catankerous old lady, expelling her dentures as she sneezes violently, without covering her nose or mouth with her handkerchief, saying "to hell with the virus and all its restrictions!" or "we may be old, but we're still full of fight" or is it a dig at the young "you make me vulnerable by not wearing a mask, here's payback, see how that feels!". Situation with Banksy is everything – viewed from a certain angle, the steep street made it seem as though the force of the old lady's sneeze was blowing houses over. A couple of fallen wheely bins, to the right of this image, added to the effect. Sadly by March 2021 the piece had been removed. It will probably reappear at auction.

WHERE?
VALE STREET,
TOTTERDOWN,
BRISTOL.

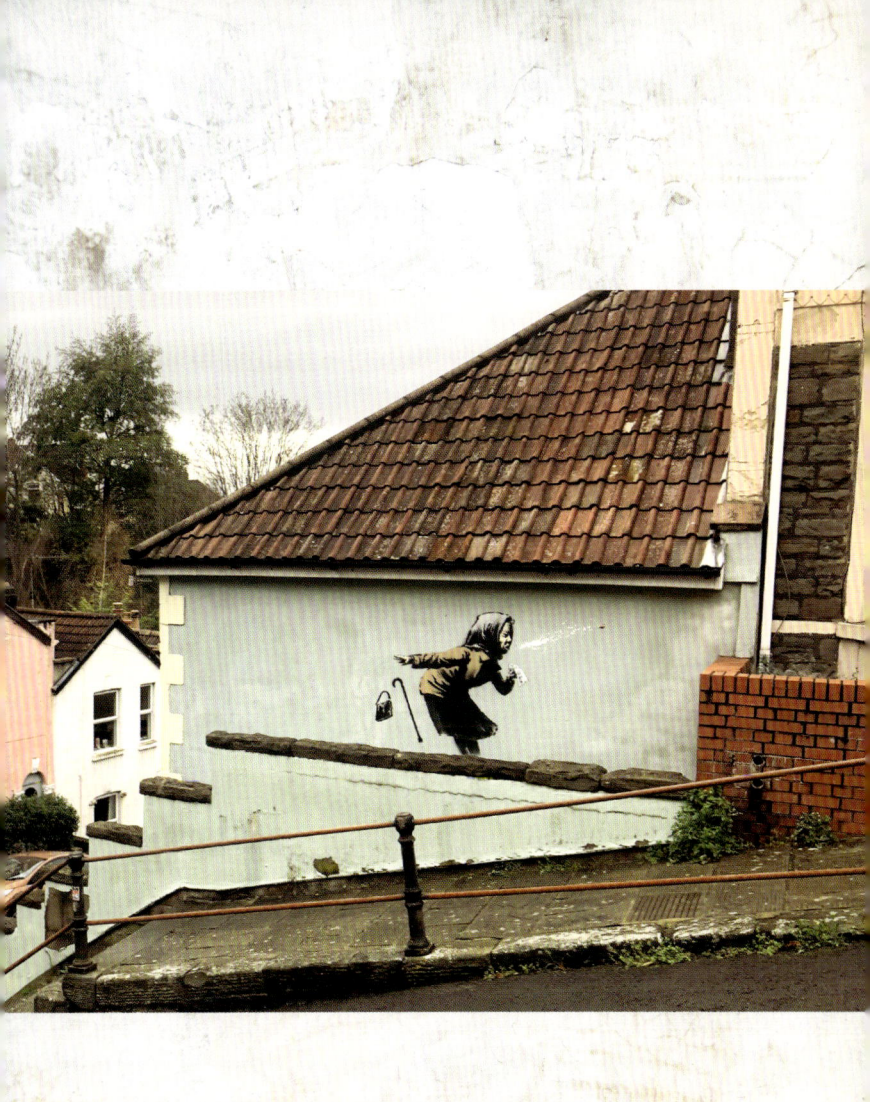

19

CREATE ESCAPE

"Society takes upon itself the right to inflict appalling punishments on the individual."
Oscar Wilde, De Profundis.

When notorious Reading Gaol closed in 2014, the philistine Tory government proposed that the site be sold to property developers. The citizens of Reading, however, wanted it turned into an arts centre. Banksy effectively threw the force of his reputation behind the latter with this brilliantly eloquent image. Its title, a pun on the classic Steve McQueen breakout movie, *The Great Escape*, suggested the gaol would be saved for the arts just in time. The escaping prisoner would seem to be a reference to Oscar Wilde. He was incarcerated here, in cell C.3.3, after being found guilty of "gross indecency" in 1895. It was here that he wrote *De Profundis* and found inspiration for his classic, *The Ballad of Reading Gaol*. The composition is typically brilliant – a heavy typewriter makes the rope made of sheets wonderfully taut. Our escapee has used the sheets as paper – a possible reference to the fact that he – the most successful playwright of his day – was initially denied pen and paper by the vindictive prison authorities. The image is a celebration of the victory of art and wit over oppressive establishments.

WHERE?
PERIMETER WALL OF READING GAOL,
READING.

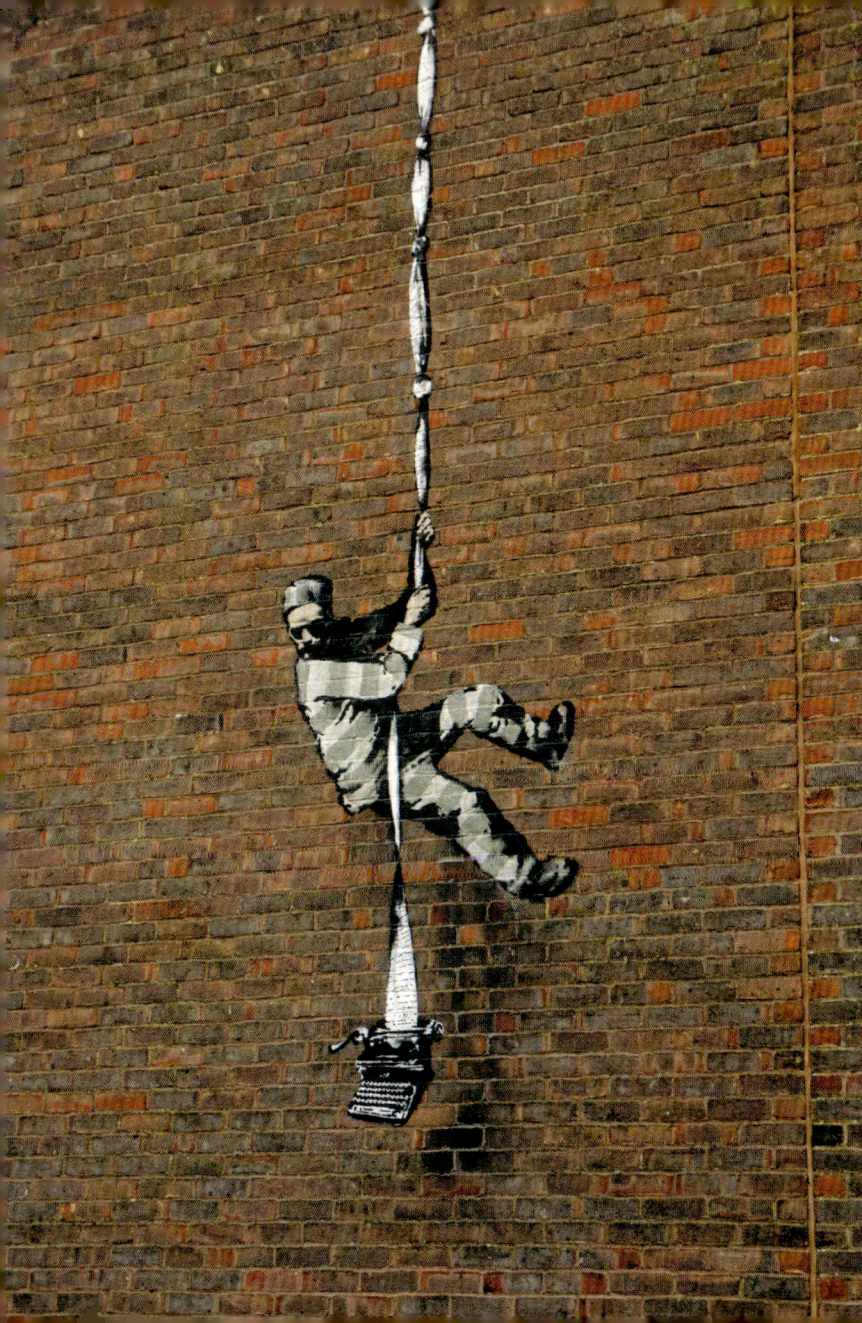

20

WE'RE ALL IN THE SAME BOAT

"I have only one eye...I really do not see the signal." **Vice Admiral Horatio Nelson, Battle of Copenhagen, 1801.**

In the summer of 2021, with Covid restrictions making international travel difficult, many Brits decided to holiday at home – what became known as having a 'staycation'. Banksy chose that August, one of the wettest on record (a pretty clear result of man-made climate change), to tour the East Anglian coast for his 'Spraycation'. This brilliant situationist piece in Lowestoft, a rather run down seaside resort, is an ironic dig at Brits moaning at not being able to holiday on sunny Mediterranean beaches, a comment on devastating flooding leading poor migrants to seek better lives (risking crossing the Channel on flimsy boats to do so) and the refusal of so many to take climate change seriously. The boy at the bow is an echo of Nelson refusing to acknowledge a signal to cease fire at the Battle of Copenhagen, by holding his telescope up to his damaged, blind eye. As usual, Banksy's child figures are filled with personality and an old-fashioned charm.

WHERE?
NICHOLAS EVERITT PARK, LOWESTOFT, SUFFOLK.

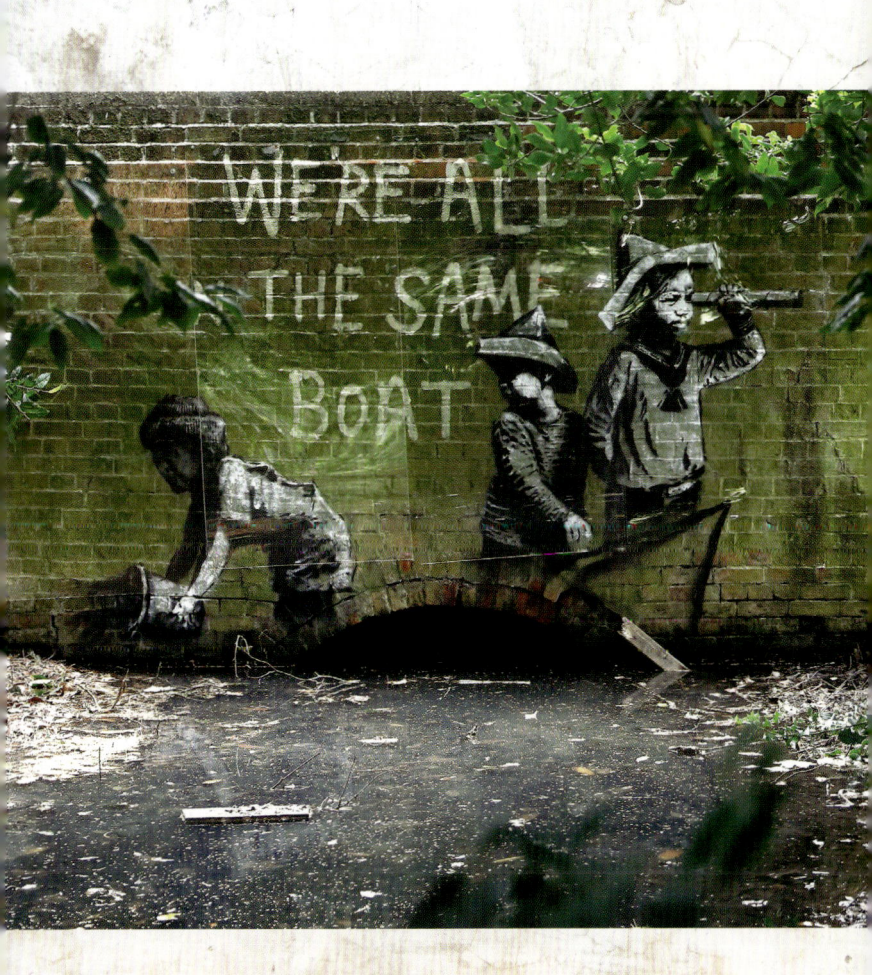

㉑

SEAGULL AND CHIPS

"Nothing is scarier than...knowing your fish and chips could fall victim to an angry seagull." Country Life

Anyone who has ever eaten fish and chips on a windswept English beach knows what a hazard swooping, screeching seagulls are as they dive to try and grab a morsel. In this brilliant piece of improvisation, Banksy, driving around Lowestoft in a battered camper van, looking for artistic opportunities, used a skip filled with discarded insulation to hilarious effect, as a representation of a chip shop container filled with chips, adding the scavenging seagull on the attack. On the surface it's a typically witty image. Yet it is also a comment on the vast amounts of useless rubbish our society produces. In a specifically British context, it also seems an oblique reference to the cladding scandal, where unsafe combustible cladding, used by unscrupulous (and profit-scavenging) developers on high–rise buildings, was a major factor in the horrific Grenfell Tower fire in 2017, in which 72 people lost their lives.

WHERE?
DENMARK WAY,
LOWESTOFT, SUFFOLK.

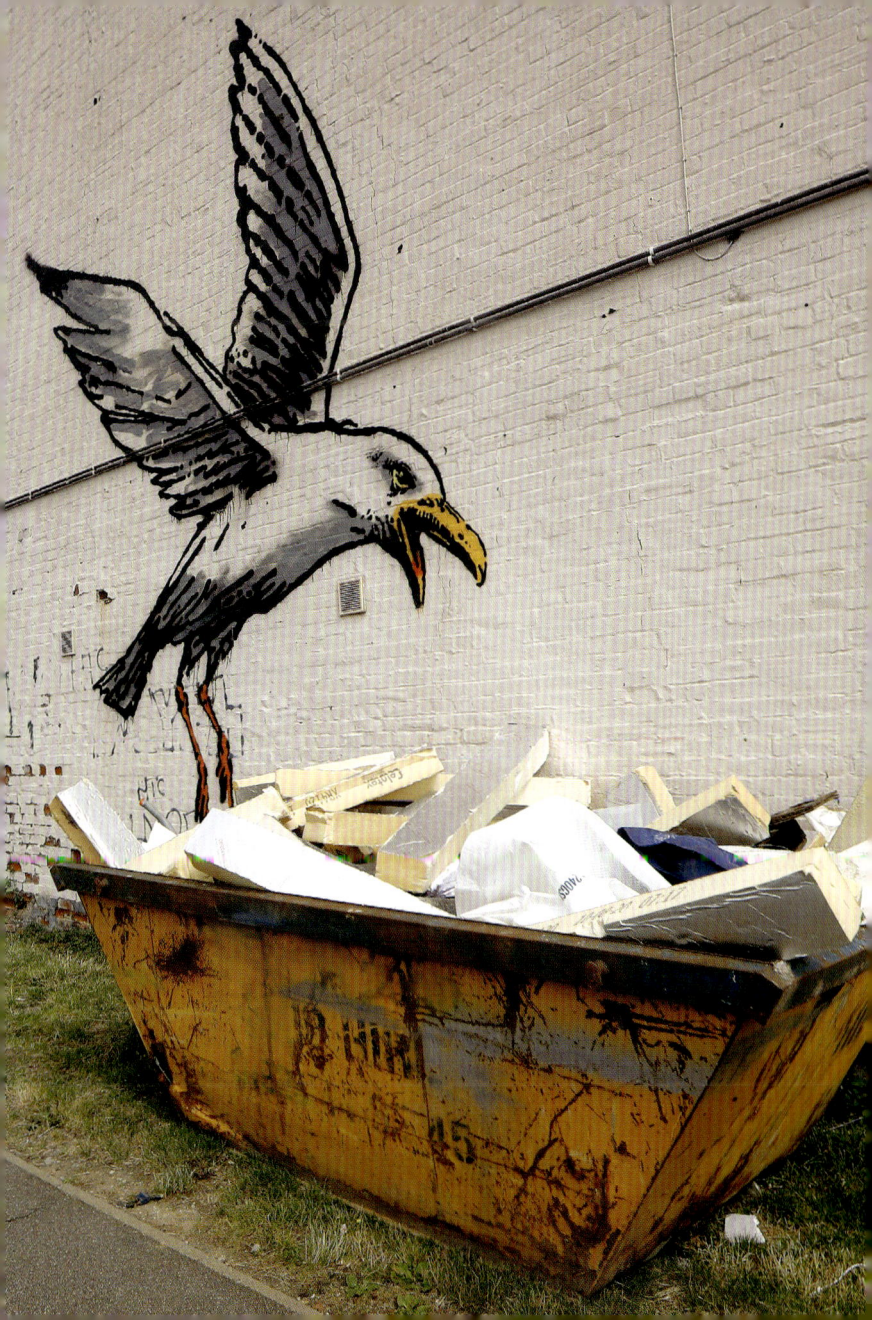

HIGH STREET SANDCASTLE

"Huge swathes of East Anglia will be under water in 30 years." Eastern Daily Press

One of the more puzzling pieces from Banksy's Spraycation, until you see it as a comment on flooding as a result of climate change. The East Anglian coast is particularly vulnerable to devastating floods, as the European Environment Agency found. Their report suggested that in a few decades, without reductions in the world's fossil fuel consumption, Lowestoft would be one of the UK towns completely under water.

As usual, Banksy creates a deeply satisfying composition, from the sand (initially formed into the shape of a castle), to the almost surreal effect of the juxtaposition of the crowbar and the concentrated, serious expression on the boy's face. Is Banksy also pointing to an intergenerational issue here? That it is our children and grandchildren who will have to deal with our inability to curb our carbon addiction?

WHERE?
LONDON ROAD NORTH,
LOWESTOFT, SUFFOLK.

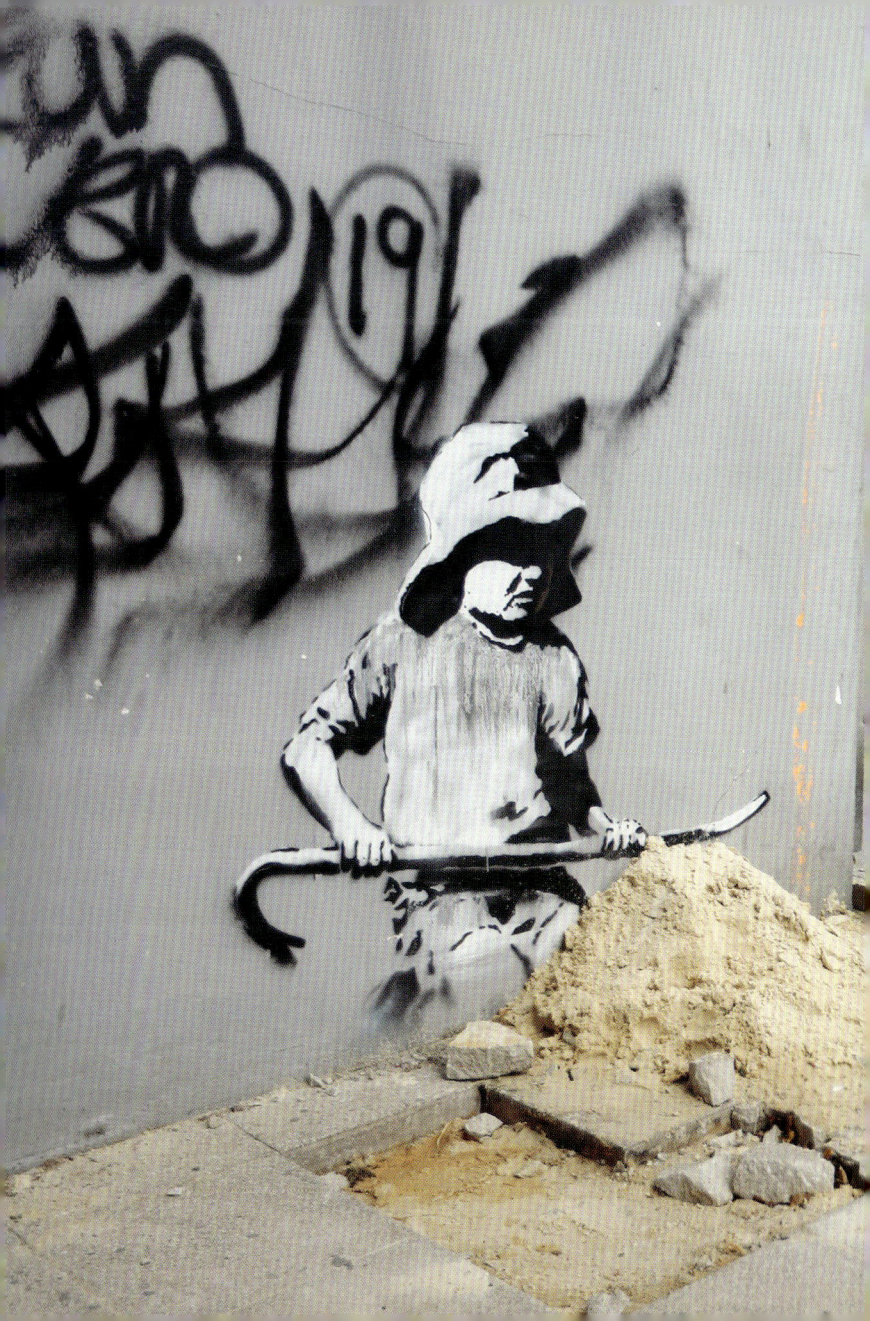

LUXURY RENTALS ONLY

"Locals have been left homeless by soaring property prices and the staycation boom."
The Times

As part of his Great British Spraycation, Banksy moved up the coast, to Cromer, a charming seaside resort increasingly a location of choice for moneyed Londoners buying holiday homes. Brilliantly, Banksy conflates this issue with a reference to the serious plight of desperate refugees, escaping wars and environmental destruction, arriving on England's shores.

This piece highlights how wealthy property owners, with their many empty properties, wish to keep new arrivals out. Banksy's attention to detail in this work is amazing. Each crab is an individual, gesturing or pleading; the crab at the rear is talking to its young. That this was painted in Cromer, renowned for the flavour of its crabs for centuries, reveals Banksy again to be a master of situation and context.

WHERE?
EAST PROM, CROMER,
NORFOLK.

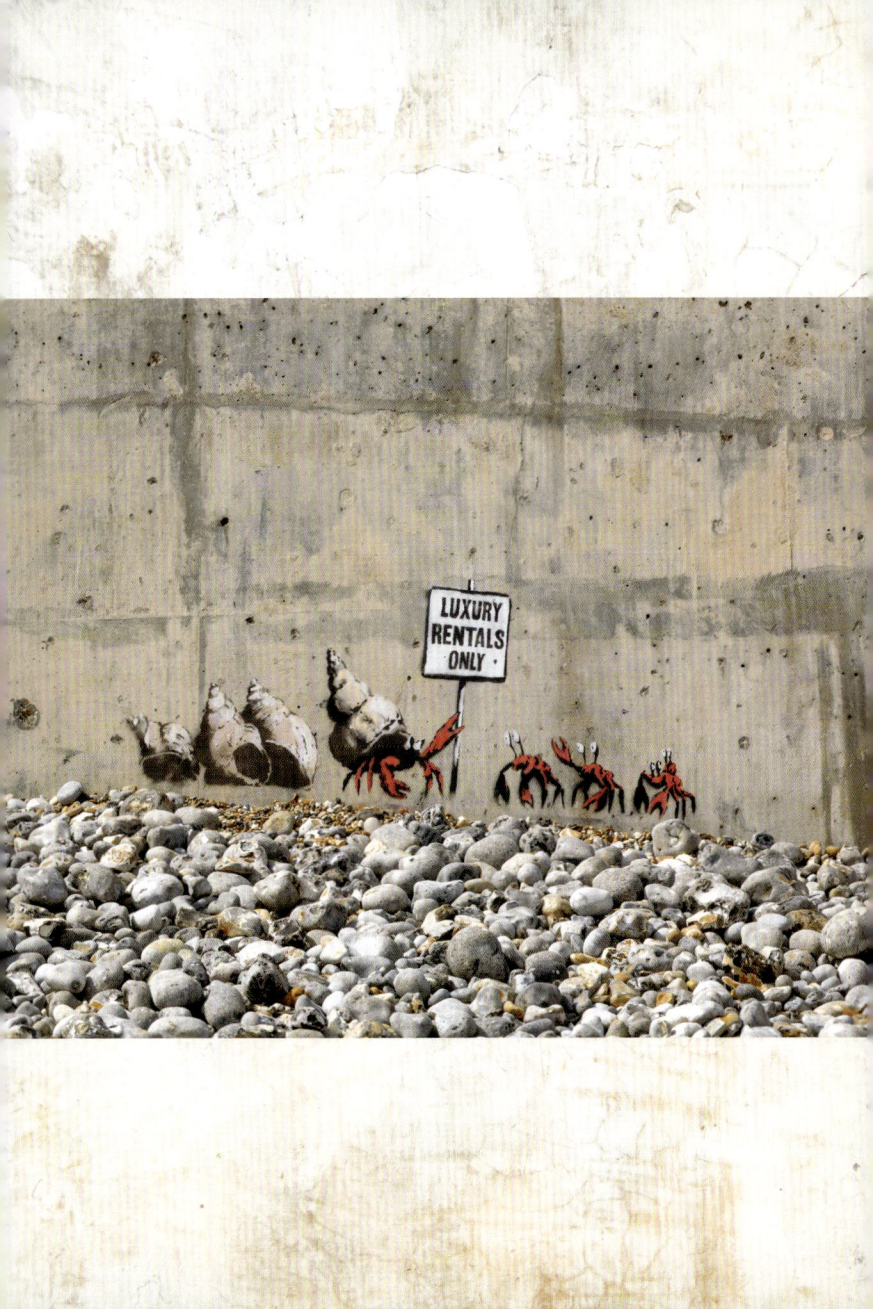

(24)

GYMNAST

"Between 20 to 30 of my neighbours were buried under the rubble." Dmytro Ostashevskyi, Borodyanka resident.

Borodyanka, a town north-west of the capital Kyiv, suffered more than most as a result of Russia's barbaric invasion of 2022. Russian troops, advancing from Belarus in February, bombarded densely populated civilian areas indiscriminately, before occupying the town. When Borodyanka was liberated in April, mass graves of civilians who had been tortured, raped and killed were found. This unbearably moving image, one of Banksy's greatest works, is a testament to the human spirit, the will to survive, and the extraordinary courage of Ukrainian people. The delicate, almost playful pose of the gymnast is in sharp contrast to the violence and horror of the collapsed apartment block. There is also an element of deep admonition. This talented child seems to be asking: how can you, the Russian government, who represent a people who love gymnastics as much as we do, allow this horror to happen? But above all there is defiance: no matter what you throw at us, our will to live will not be extinguished.

WHERE?
COLLAPSED APARTMENT BLOCK,
BORODYANKA.

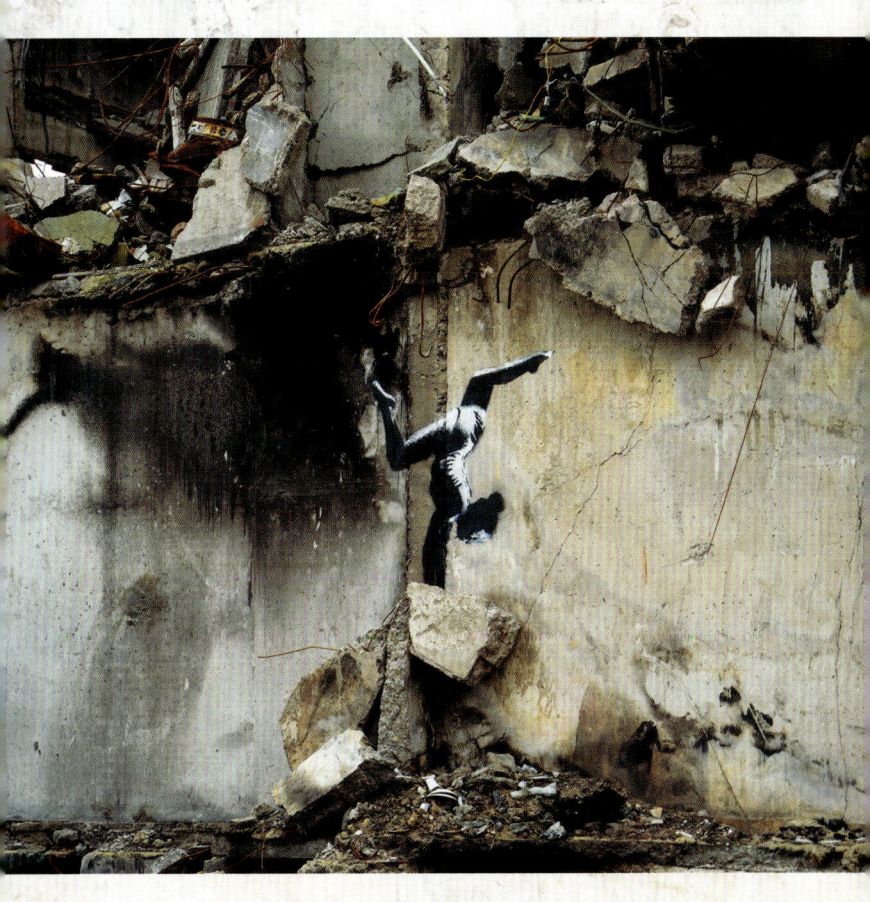

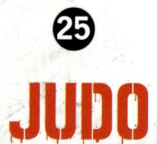

JUDO

"Putin is a Judoka and these actions are against the spirit and purpose of Judo."
Yasuhiro Yamashita, All Japan Judo Federation.

Vladimir Putin liked to prove his macho credentials with displays of Judo (in which he held a black belt) and on an instructional video, *Let's Learn Judo with Vladimir Putin,* for the faithful. In this hilarious take on the David and Goliath story, a much younger, nimble, youthful lad (Ukraine), effortlessly throws a lumbering clumsy old guy way past his prime (Putin/ Russia) to the ground. As ever with Banksy, the symbolism runs deep. As a comment on the progress of the war, it is brilliant – Russia was inept, tactically deficient and clearly losing by November 2022 when this appeared. There is a nod to Putin's black belt. Notwithstanding this, the dishonour that Putin visited on the noble traditions of Judo led to him being stripped of all his titles by the International Judo Federation in March 2022, for his invasion of Ukraine and obscene violence against civilians. A week earlier World Taekwondo had stripped Putin of his honorary black belt, stating that Russia's attack on Ukraine went against the values of Taekwondo, which state that "Peace is more precious than triumph."

WHERE?
BOMBED OUT APARTMENT BUILDING,
BORODYANKA.

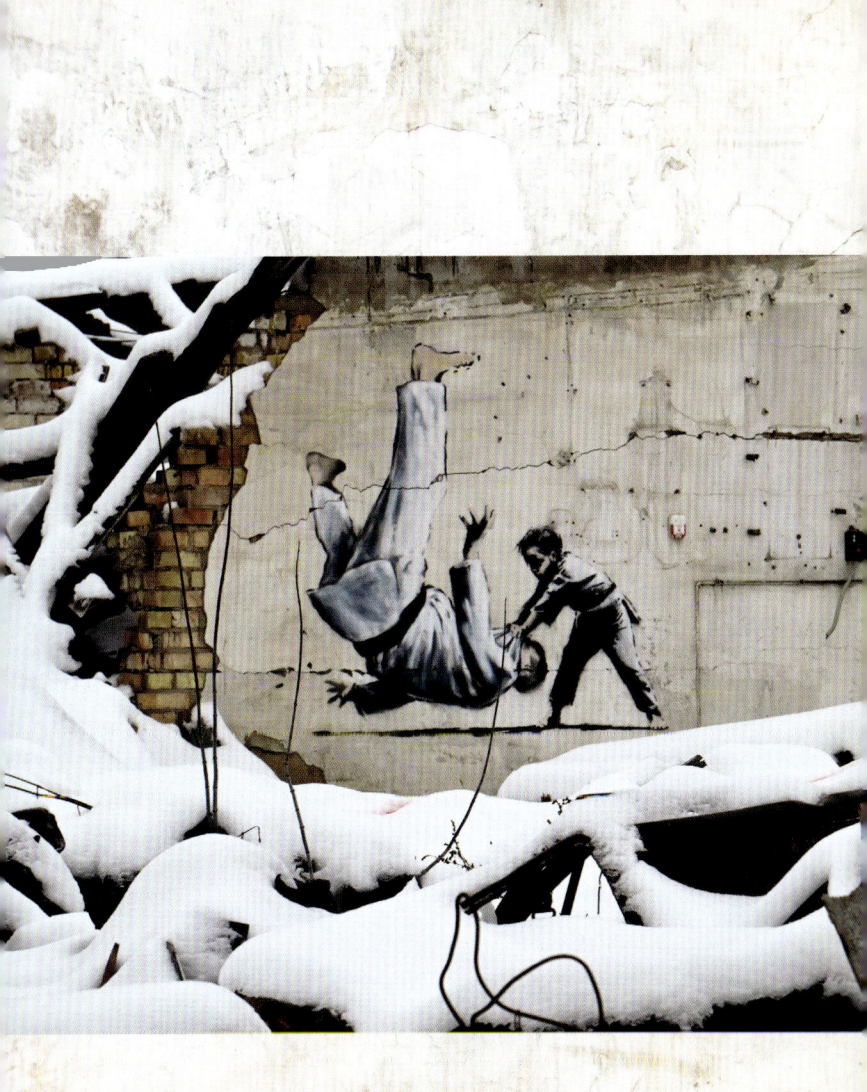

WOMAN IN CURLERS

"These images are a symbol of our struggle against the enemy." **Oleksii Kuleba, Governor of Kyiv Oblast.**

A bombed out apartment building in Hostomel, to the noth-west of Kyiv. We don't know how many died as a result of Russian troops attacking civilian areas here. Banksy has used the mustard coloured wall as the perfect canvas for another unforgetable image of civilian defiance. The woman in her dressing gown, with curlers in her hair, has clearly been interrupted, probably in her morning routine; notwithstanding the war, she won't change her habits. The fire extinguisher and gas mask point to a practical, no nonsense, unflappable response. The use of the chair shows the woman standing tall: this is not a population whose spirit will be broken. There is an echo here of images of the London Blitz during the Second World War: the dressing gown, curlers and retro gas mask are straight out of London's East End, circa 1941. Is this a suggestion from Banksy that this pointless war is the worst since 1945, and that Putin's aggression is on a par with that of the Nazis?

WHERE?
BOMBED OUT APARTMENT BUILDING,
RESIDENTIAL NEIGHBOURHOOD,
HOSTOMEL.

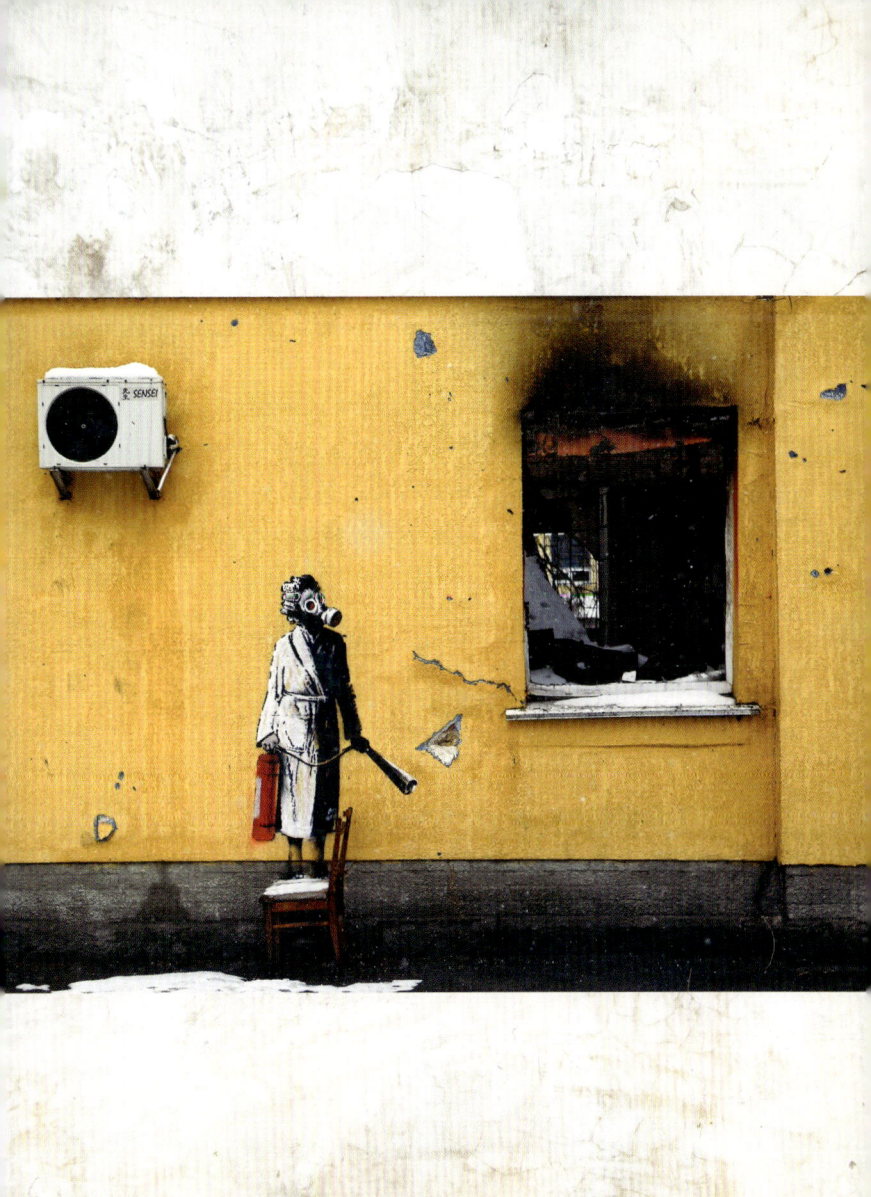

CREDITS

This book was made possible by the many photographers around the world who have documented Banksy's work. Apart from their evident enthusiasm for this most brilliant of street artists, they have ensured a valuable record of his work as seen on the street, usually before it has been buffed, defaced or otherwise destroyed. We are particularly grateful to our headline team, Kevin Flemen, Ross Holdsworth, Lord Jim, Canis Major, Sam Martin and Allan Molho. Without their enthusiasm, this volume would not exist.

Credits are listed below by name of work, in the order they appear in the book:

EARLY WORKS
Mild Mild West
CANIS MAJOR
Gorilla in a Pink Mask
CANIS MAJOR
Always Hope
KEVIN FLEMEN

2003-2004
Grim Reaper
CANIS MAJOR
Flower Thower
GOETZE-IMAGES.COM
Kissing Coppers
KEVIN FLEMEN
Because I'm Worthless
KEVIN FLEMEN
What are you looking At?
NOLIFEBEFORECOFFEE

2005-2006
Guantanamo
KEVIN FLEMEN
Snorting Copper
SAM MARTIN
Boy at the Beach
MARCO DI LAURO/ GETTY IMAGES
Well Hung Lover
PHILIP CERVI
Sweeping it Under the Carpet
FLICKR/KRIEBEL

2007-2008
Vandalism is Art
KEVIN FLEMEN
ATM
KEVIN FLEMEN

Yellow Lines Flower Painter
KEVIN FLEMEN
Caveman
LORD JIM
One Nation Under CCTV
SAM MARTIN
Let Them Eat Crack
ALLAN MOLHO

2009-2010
No Fishing
SAM MARTIN
Exit Through The Gift Shop
EVERETT/REX/ SHUTTERSTOCK
Guard On Duty
LORD JIM
Park
LORD JIM
Tesco Sand Castles
SAM MARTIN
Call an Airstrke
FLICKR.COM/THE STIG2009
I Love NY
ALLAN MOLHO

2011-2012
Firestarter
LORD JIM
Crayola Shooter
LORD JIM
Slave Labour
FLICKR/DEPTFORDJON
The Lifestyle You Ordered
ROSS HOLDSWORTH

2013 THE NEW YORK RESIDENCY
The Street is in Play
ALLAN MOLHO
Ghetto 4 Life
ALLAN MOLHO
Waiting in Vain
ALLAN MOLHO
Japanese Scene
ALLAN MOLHO
Shoe Shine Boy
ALLAN MOLHO
Sirens of the Lambs
ALLAN MOLHO
What We Do in Life
ALLAN MOLHO
Echoes in Eternity
ALLAN MOLHO
Os Gemeos Collaboration
ALLAN MOLHO

RECENT WORKS
Girl With a Pierced Ear Drum
CANIS MAJOR
Eavesdropping
PHILIP CERVI
Dismaland
LUCAS ROSS
Son of a Syrian Refugee
RICK FINDLER/REX/ SHUTTERSTOCK
Kitten
NURPHOTO/REX/ SHUTTERSTOCK
Cosette
TOLGA AKMEN/LNP/REX/ SHUTTERSTOCK

Bridge Farm Primary School
REX/SHUTTERSTOCK
Walled-off Hotel Exterior
HASHLAMOUN/EPA/REX/ SHUTTERSTOCK
Rage – The Flower Thrower 2
HASHLAMOUN/ EPA/ REX/ SHUTTERSTOCK
Breaking News
LEVINE/ SIPA/ REX/ SHUTTERSTOCK
Brexit SAM MILLEN
Basquiat PAUL MENDOZA
Refugee Girl
PIERRE-ETIENNE AUROUSSEAU
Crossing the Alps
PIERRE-ETIENNE AUROUSSEAU
Love is in the Bin
ALAMY
Venice in Oil ALAMY
Devolved Parliament
ALAMY
Aachoo!! ALAMY
Create Escape ALAMY
We're All in the Same Boat ALAMY
Seagull and Chips
ALAMY
High Street Sandcastle
ALAMY
Luxury Rentals Only
ALAMY
Gymnast ALAMY
Judo ALAMY
Woman in Curlers ALAMY

First Published in the United States of America, May 2023. Gingko Press, 2332 Fourth Street, Suite E, Berkeley, CA 94710, USA.
Published under license from Graffito Books
ISBN 978-1-58423-769-3
Printed in China
© Graffito Books Ltd, 2023. www.graffitobooks.com.

This is not an official publication. This is also an unauthorised work examining the political and social background to the foremost street art polemicist of our dystopian age. However, the mysterious, enigmatic and hidden artist who creates under the moniker BANKSY had no part in its inception or creation. The contents, analysis and interpretations within express the views and opinions of Graffito Books Ltd only. All images in this book have been produced with the knowledge and prior consent of the photographers concerned.

Art Director: Karen Wilks
Research Editor: Lucy Radford-Earle